# The First Macedonian Colony

## The Untold History of the Macedonian Settlement in Granite City

Victor Sinadinoski

*Macedonians of America Series*

Copyright © 2019 by Victor Sinadinoski
All rights reserved. This book or any portion thereof may not be reproduced or used in any manner whatsoever without the express written permission of the publisher except for the use of brief quotations.

Printed in the United States of America

ISBN: 978-1795342872

For my brother, Dean.

# PART I

# An Extraordinary Life

# ONE
# The Death of Sarafov

At the dawn of the 20th century, Turkish oppression in Macedonia was being challenged by a formidable revolutionary force known as the Internal Macedonian Revolutionary Organization (IMRO). This ambitious secret society was overcrowded with impressive figures. Founded by teachers and intellectuals in 1893, it steadily became infused with bandits, peasants, mercenaries, merchants, priests, children, and women. Anyone who dreamed of freedom from the Sultan's clutch and the establishment of a 'Macedonia for the Macedonians' carved a path into IMRO's ranks.

One such revolutionary was Boris Sarafov, perhaps the most unpredictable, perplexing and magnetic character of the Macedonian liberation movement. As a child, Sarafov witnessed his father and grandfather hauled through the streets of Solun[1] as punishment for their political agitation, an event that "shook Sarafov's soul and...shaped his future activities."[2] The young Macedonian swore revenge on the Turkish Empire. He moved to sovereign Bulgaria, joined the military, and in 1896 was elected president of the Supreme Macedonian-Adrianople Committee,[3] a Macedonian organization formed in Bulgaria that openly advocated for Macedonia's freedom and was informally considered a tool of Bulgaria's Prince Ferdinand. For several years, Sarafov would lead bands of Macedonians and Bulgarians into Macedonia, stirring up some trouble and then leaving peasants to their own devices once the Sultan's troops caught wind of his presence.

Sarafov's slippery allegiances tarnished his credibility with IMRO's leaders. He sometimes aligned with the autonomists, such as Goce Delchev and Jane Sandanski, who relentlessly advocated for Macedonia's independence and the uniqueness of the Macedonians. Once, during a conversation with Delchev, Sarafov offered to assassinate a leader of the anti-autonomist Macedonians after Sarafov was sidelined from that faction.[4] To a London newspaper, Sarafov proclaimed that "Macedonians consider ourselves to be an entirely separate national element, and we are not in the least disposed to allow our country to be seized by Bulgaria, Servia, or Greece…Macedonia must belong to the Macedonians."[5] An abundance of records exist detailing his assertions of his Macedonian identity and desire to establish an independent Macedonia.

Other times Sarafov joined with the forces of Prince Ferdinand, who coveted Macedonia as an extension of his Bulgarian kingdom. His shiftiness was highlighted by Hristo Uzunov, a leading IMRO figure in western Macedonia, who penned a letter on his deathbed asking fellow IMRO leaders to "annihilate as soon as possible those hitherto leading forces in the Organization who have inflicted damage upon the Cause, like Sarafov[.]"[6] Arthur D.H. Smith, in his 1908 book, *Fighting the Turk in the Balkans*, summed up Sarafov's role in the Macedonian liberation movement by exclaiming that Sarafov was a paid spy for Prince Ferdinand and his head pawn in controlling the progress of the Macedonian revolution.[7]

Still, Sarafov maintained a considerable following amongst Macedonians throughout Europe and America. If Delchev was the soul of the Macedonian liberation movement, then Sarafov was undoubtedly the image of the movement to the outside world, even though he was less popular within Macedonia.[8] Unlike most revolutionaries, Sarafov spent relatively little time inside enslaved Macedonia. Contrary to IMRO's principles, he enticed impressionable young Macedonian men to join his ranks by paying them "princely salaries" so they could afford "fine clothes and other luxuries," and these Macedonians based their operations out of Bulgaria.[9] Many of Sarafov's other adventures consisted of touring Europe, raising money (often by extracting it through threats and blackmail), and speaking on behalf of the subjugated Macedonian people.

Not only did Sarafov unearth a platform in Europe to preach against the injustices of Turkish occupation, he also found the pockets of businessmen and the ears of politicians. He targeted wealthy capitalists in Vienna's casinos and prominent European politicians in Paris.[10] Further, he concocted many wild strategies for winning over Macedonia's freedom. For example, he attempted to raise a loan of several million dollars from British politicians in exchange for guaranteeing Britain's right to exploit Macedonia's natural resources once Macedonia was freed.[11] He offered to supply the United States with hundreds of Macedonian soldiers during the Spanish-American war in exchange for money and weapons,[12] and he threatened to release the plague in Turkish cities if the Sultan ignored the Macedonians' demands.[13] Because of these bold announcements and his snug relationships with foreign journalists, businessmen and politicians, the Macedonian liberation movement and Sarafov became one and the same for the European and American press during the first decade of the 20th century.

Thus, it is unsurprising that the American press speculated that Sarafov landed in America in the summer of 1907 and slipped by immigration officials using a fake name. His destination, said the press, was the Macedonian capital of America: Granite City.[14]

Granite City, located in Illinois on the east side of the Mississippi River across from St. Louis, was founded in 1896 by two brothers who desired to establish a new location for their graniteware factory, which was one of the largest granite enameling companies in the world.[15] Frederick and William Niedringhaus bought 4,000 acres in 1893 and three years later incorporated that land into Granite City. Their National Enameling and Stamping Company was eventually joined by American Steel Foundries and Commonwealth Steel Company, as well as other factories. These factories required thousands of unskilled workers.[16] By the summer of 1907, several thousand Macedonians were employed at these factories in Granite City.[17] How this many Macedonians ended up in the middle of America is a remarkable story that will be told later in this book. For now, however, it is enough to know that Sarafov would have had good reason to visit Granite City.

Not only was Granite City swarming with Macedonians, but many of these Macedonians viewed Sarafov as their leader. Certainly, many others detested him and would have rather lived under Turkish occupation than see Sarafov become Macedonia's leader; however, a sizeable Granite City faction of Macedonians admired him and were deemed some of his most ardent followers outside of the Balkans.[18] While in Granite City, Sarafov acquainted himself with the Macedonian population, was implicated in an attempted assassination on a Greek, and collected $35,000 in contributions from the Macedonian laborers for IMRO's war chest.[19] In today's value, that amounts to nearly $900,000, an astronomical figure given that most Macedonians in Granite City worked low-wage jobs, which paid between $1.50 and $2.50 per day (roughly between $40 and $70 in today's value).[20]

Sarafov's visit to Illinois was not corroborated by many sources, but his misuse of the funds acquired there and throughout Europe is abundantly documented. Christo Nedelkoff, editor of the *Naroden Glas* (a Macedonian newspaper published in Granite City)[21] and a Sarafov supporter, explained the dilemma surrounding the missing funds to the American press:

> He was accustomed to collect large sums in contributions from Macedonians, which were spent for firearms and other revolutionary equipment in the necessary work of smuggling them in. In the recent Macedonian Congress, or revolutionary convention, at Sofia, it was charged that Sarafoff had failed to account for several thousand *francs* collected by him. Sarafoff admitted that there was money unaccounted for, but said he would explain where the money went if the congress would pledge itself to secrecy. This was done. It is not known exactly how he explained the matter, but it is generally supposed that he said the money was used in bribing Turkish officials in Macedonia.[22]

Others painted a different picture of what happened to the funds. Arthur Smith wrote that it was conclusively proven Sarafov had embezzled $100,000 ($2.5 million in today's value), but that no one dared move against him because he was under Prince Ferdinand's protection.[23] The American wife of self-proclaimed Serbian Prince Eugene Lazarovich-

Hrebelianovich met Sarafov in London and claimed that Sarafov was devoting donated funds toward his own ends, hoping that a successful Macedonian insurrection would earn him a high-ranked political position in Bulgaria. "He did his work well for Bulgaria," she noted.[24]

Whether or not the source of missing funds was the underlying source of anger for Sarafov's opponents or simply just one of many reasons to not trust the conniving revolutionary, this debacle was the last lick for the Macedonian autonomists. Jane Sandanski, the legendary Macedonian who fought against Bulgarian intrusion into the Macedonian revolutionary movement just as hard as he fought against the Sultan's reign, vowed that this would be Sarafov's final betrayal of the Macedonian people. He could no longer tolerate Sarafov's methods. "You fight and run away," he told Sarafov, "leaving the peasants here to suffer undefended at the hands of the Turks."[25]

Thus, in December of 1907, Sarafov was assassinated by Todor Panica, a Sandanski loyalist, who put a bullet in Sarafov's head after making his acquaintance and feigning admiration for Sarafov's goals and methods.[26] In February of 1908, Sandanski penned an open letter explaining the assassination of Sarafov. He claimed the murder was "an act of justice" because Sarafov had been sentenced to death by a revolutionary tribunal. The organization possessed many documents proving Sarafov's treachery, said Sandanski. In particular, the documents demonstrated that Sarafov had, on numerous occasions, planned attempted assassinations on Sandanski and his loyalists in order to gain control over Macedonia's Serres district. Sandanski warned that Sarafov's fate would reach all who followed Sarafov's example. He proclaimed Serres to be the IMRO's last stronghold and that he would prevent the poison of Bulgarian nationalism from infecting the district.[27]

Following Sarafov's assassination, the Macedonians in Granite City and neighboring cities (such as Madison, Venice and St. Louis) became greatly agitated. They held small gatherings in their communities to honor his memory and discuss the events surrounding the assassination. Some desired a larger religious service to honor him, but construction of the Macedonian-Bulgarian Orthodox Church[28] in Granite City was not yet complete and they had no priest in Illinois.[29]

Over a year later, Macedonians in Granite City still bore bitterness over the assassination of Sarafov and the fracturing of the Macedonian liberation movement. In an ironic twist, Macedonians unleashed their anger on Bulgarians in Granite City, even though their admired Sarafov had been damned for serving Bulgaria's interests. Throughout 1908, occasional bar fights and street skirmishes disturbed the fragile peace between the Macedonians and Bulgarians. One newspaper noted that the tension was even visible in the factories, where "for several months there [had] been intense rivalry between the Macedonians and Bulgarians." This tension culminated on the weekend of President Abraham Lincoln's Centennial Celebration (February 12, 1909), a celebration marking the 100th year since Lincoln's birth.[30]

The factories were closed that Friday and Granite City's immigrant laborers had retreated into the saloons of Hungary Hollow, a section of Granite City where Hungarians, Macedonians, Bulgarians and other immigrants had established an enclave for themselves. At a Macedonian-owned saloon, the different groups of immigrants were segregated into their own sections but generally well-behaved. Some Macedonians had engaged in a light-hearted discussion comparing the legacies of Sarafov and Lincoln, when they were interrupted by a Bulgarian named George. George had overheard the conversation from his table, and in his inebriated state, interjected with his thoughts. "Lincoln was a great man," said George, "and a patriot who did things. Your renegade Sarafov was not. Sarafov said he would free the slaves of Macedonia, but he did not." This audacious utterance greatly perturbed the Macedonians. The IMRO movement to free Macedonia had not succeeded and the Macedonians were still second-class citizens in their own land. These Sarafov supporters would not think of attributing Macedonia's enslavement to Sarafov's failures. A heated exchange between the men ensued, but cooler heads in the saloon managed to prevent a fight.[31]

Sunday was not a day of rest in Granite City, and the American Steel Foundry rekindled operations two days after the dispute between the Bulgarians and the Macedonians. Neutral observers that morning noticed that the Macedonians and Bulgarians had gathered in different sections of the plant and seemed greatly agitated. As soon as the whistle sounded, signaling the start of the work day, a group of over 100 Macedonians charged a slightly smaller posse of Bulgarians, who had surely anticipated a fight. What happened next was described as "race animosity, fanned by the discussion of a chance remark in a saloon."[32]

Over 200 men armed with stones, knives, iron bars and everything but firearms clashed in the foundry. For several minutes, the Macedonians and Bulgarians battled out their hatred for another. Bonzi Ivan was stabbed in the head; Barca Conreff was sliced on the back and the head; Jaco Kronzeff was bleeding from stab wounds to his stomach; Leopold Conir suffered a concussion after a blow to the head; and dozens more were recipients of bloody noses, black eyes, scrapes and bruises. But as quickly as the fight began, it came to a halt with the screeches of Anthony, the Bulgarian leader, who screamed out in agonizing pain that he was dying. He had been stabbed several times in the back and knocked down to the ground by a direct hit to his head.[33]

Like in many old-school brawls, the fight ended when the leader went down; in this case, the Bulgarians' leader was bleeding to death. The groups cautiously retreated to their corners. They attempted to begin their foundry duties, but soon the Granite City police flooded the factory. The Macedonians dispersed and took their wounded back to Hungary Hollow.[34]

This fight was over, for now, and the Bulgarians had hopefully learned their lesson. However, the Greeks – historical enemies of the Macedonians – in Granite City and neighboring cities had much more to worry about. A secret Macedonian society based in Granite City had bigger fish to fry than out-of-place Bulgarians, and the Greeks knew that the Bulgarians were merely a distraction for the Macedonians; they knew the Macedonians were out to settle unfinished business that was rooted in the homeland.

# TWO
# The Black Hand

While the Macedonians and Bulgarians occasionally clashed in Granite City, the predominant ethnic battle in southwestern Illinois and St. Louis during the early 20th century was between the Greeks and the Macedonians. The Greek consuls in America accused the Macedonians of operating a secret Macedonian society (which they referred to as the 'Black Hand') with headquarters in Granite City. This society, said the Greeks, would blackmail Greeks, Bulgarians and even Macedonians throughout America into contributing funds to their organization. Those funds were then used to advance IMRO's agenda in Macedonia: the creation of an independent Macedonia. These funds were extracted, according to some, by threatening to murder an individual or his family members in the Balkans should he not pay the ransom. The Greeks asserted that between 1903 and 1907, over 150 Greeks, Macedonians and Bulgarians in the U.S. had been murdered by this society.[35]

Some Macedonians confirmed the existence of such a group. Others, however, viewed this as an official Greek smear campaign against the Macedonians in order to discredit their fight for freedom. Like Bulgaria and Serbia, Greece desired to annex Macedonia: the whole land, if possible, but the southernmost areas would be acceptable. The IMRO opposed any division of Macedonia and insisted on the establishment of an autonomous Macedonia, free from foreign rule. Many Macedonians in America therefore rallied to the defense of those Macedonians branded by the Greeks as criminals, claiming that the accusations were a political ruse aimed at satisfying the chauvinistic appetite of the Greek government. The American press blasted both the Macedonians and Greeks for bringing "their feuds to America, where they think liberty is license and that they can stab, shoot and assassinate like the Craigs, the Tellivers, the Hatfields and the Hargises."[36]

The apparent mastermind of this Macedonian operation was Sougar Roumaneff, also known as Steven Roucheff, but commonly referred to as Gospodar and Janos Grastus. These two nicknames reveal clues to Roumaneff's importance and standing in the Macedonian community without even delving into his background. For example, in Macedonian, *gospodar* is roughly equivalent to *master* or *manager*. It refers to someone who is wise, skilled and competent with his affairs, and has control over people and things. We can thus infer that Roumaneff was some sort of boss in this Macedonian 'Black Hand.'

His other nickname, Janos Grastus, sends a different message. *Janos* is simply the Hungarian variant of *John* (or the Macedonian *Jovan*) and at first glance appears to simply be a code name. However, *Grastus*, although sounding like a Hungarian surname to untrained ears, is not a typical Hungarian name. As a matter of fact, Roumaneff knew that it sounded Hungarian and used it in order to detract authorities from uncovering his true identity. When he was first detained by police, he insisted that he was Hungarian.[37] But why choose *Grastus* when there exist actual Hungarian surnames? Perhaps he assumed it sounded Hungarian enough to deceive the unsuspecting.

Yet, maybe it is likely Roumaneff also chose *Grastus* for another reason: its symbolism. In ancient history, Grastus is known as the son of King Mygdon, the founder of the Mygdonia region in ancient Macedonia[38] (some historians even suggest that ancient Macedonia was named after Mygdonia). Grastus was thought to have established the Krestonia region in Macedonia, north of Mygdonia,[39] which roughly corresponds to an area just south of Kukush,[40] where IMRO leader, Goce Delchev, was born. Furthermore, Roumaneff was from eastern Macedonia (which includes Kukush). Could this be another reason he used the code name Grastus, or was it just a coincidence? Did Roumaneff intend for the code name *Janos Grastus* to have a double meaning, one to sidetrack authorities from his true identity and another to emphasize his Macedonian identity and his connection to the ancient Macedonians?

While we do not have an answer to that question, we do know that Roumaneff was a man of influence among the Macedonians. In the mid-1890s, he had led bands of Macedonians on raids into the northern districts of Macedonia.[41] For ten years he injected himself into the Macedonian revolutionary movement until a Turkish reward for his capture or execution motivated him to flee Macedonia – at least this was the story according to Greek officials.[42] A cablegram from Turkish officials in Bitola, Macedonia later revealed that Roumaneff was unknown of in western Macedonia and that he was likely an agent of the Macedonian committee based out of Sofia.[43] Roumaneff eventually admitted that he was a member of a secret society in Macedonia that was responsible for unrest and disturbances in Turkish Macedonia, but he did not confirm that he had fled Turkey for this reason.[44] Nevertheless, a Greek official in America, George Tsolomiti (Greek vice-consul based in Butte, Montana[45] and representative of the interests of the Greeks in the Pacific Northwest),[46] notified Greek consuls throughout the country in the spring of 1906 that Roumaneff had arrived in St. Louis sometime in 1905, and that Greek and American officials should be watchful for his presence.[47]

From his arrival in 1905 until his arrest in December of 1906, the Granite City's 'Gospodar' was accused by the Greeks of orchestrating the murder of 100 Balkan immigrants and the successful blackmailing of many times more that number.[48] This criminal operation extended from California to Texas and across the country to the shores of the Atlantic, although the bulk of its activity centered in Illinois, Indiana and Ohio, where there were significant Balkan communities. Still, allegations of this cross-country mafia-styled scheme were not insignificant. The Greek consuls deemed this 'Black Hand' liable for the murders of six in Minneapolis, three in San Francisco, two in Indianapolis, one in Port Lavaca, Texas and many more in New York.[49]

However, all instances of murder and blackmail cases prior to Roumaneff's arrest in December of 1906 had remained unresolved and inconclusively connected to any organized Macedonian attempt to extract funds for the Macedonian liberation movement. The murder of six Macedonians in Minneapolis, which was the highest number of Macedonians murdered at once, remains unsolved even today. While some theorize it was just a horrific robbery, most police officers were adamant that it was the work of the Macedonian 'Black Hand'.[50]

Eleven Macedonians were initially arrested for the crime but there was inconclusive evidence connecting them to the murders.[51] Even though one of the men had blood stains on his clothes, the police released the Macedonians. Two fled Minnesota and were last spotted in Chicago, where some witnesses indicated the men had escaped to either New York or Seattle.[52]

Moreover, a letter written in Macedonian was found at the crime scene. The police interviewed several dozen Macedonians in hopes of unraveling its contents. But they had no luck. "They'd stare at it a few minutes," said one detective, "and then shake their heads, pleading that if they told us what was in there they wouldn't live long."[53] About seven months later, a Macedonian who had lived in the house and who volunteered information on the six victims, was discovered floating in a river two blocks from the location of the mass murder. Police concluded that he was killed and thrown into the river because seven of his toes had been amputated, there was no water in his lungs, and his hands were cut in several places, indicating a struggle. Some Macedonians had previously warned police that he would be the next to die because he too was entangled in the Macedonian vendetta.[54] Greeks in the area linked the murder to Roumaneff and the 'Black Hand' headquartered in Granite City, but the police had no evidence to connect them to the murder.[55]

In another instance, the Greek officials associated an assassination attempt on a Greek working in Maysville, Kentucky to Naum Demetri, a Macedonian who had once lived in Granite City. Supposedly, when Roumaneff had discovered that the plot to murder the Greek in Kentucky failed and that the victim, Thomas James, was pressing charges against Demetri, he sent word to Macedonia. Macedonians there murdered James' father, cut his body into four quarters and strung his body parts on a tree in his village for all peasants to see.[56]

The police arrested Demetri but were unable to extract information from him because he possessed no knowledge of English. They did find a revolver on him, and the bullets in the revolved matched that which had been lodged in James' neck.[57] While Demetri lingered in jail, James told the police that the Macedonian 'Black Hand' continued to threaten his life. "I want permission to carry a revolver," he said. His attorney then presented police with letters written by the secret Macedonian society that had been sent to other Greeks in Maysville.[58]

Macedonians insisted that this attempted assassination had no connection to any secret society. Instead, they claimed it was revenge for the rape of Demetri's wife in Macedonia. Around the same time (autumn of 1906) that Demetri received a letter from Macedonia detailing the rape, he had lost his job working with a construction gang, of which James was the foreman. He blamed James for his job loss and associated him with the conspiracy to ruin his life. The *Public Ledger* wrote:

**From that time he planned revenge. William Stammatt, Macedonian baker at Front and Plum streets, says Naoum bought a big knife. He showed it and said it was to take the life of James. Then he planned to go back to Macedonia to levy revenge on the men who had soiled his home. ... "They have brought shame to my home and now they conspire to ruin me," Naoum declared.[59]**

A little closer to home, in Chicago, Macedonians were suspected of having murdered Zincenz Glocentios, a Greek and section foreman for a railroad company. Glocentios had left work for the grocery store in order to buy provisions for his section. During his return trip, he was fired upon by three men. Three Macedonian section members were arrested but shortly thereafter released due to a lack of proof.[60]

The 150 unsolved murder cases in America constituted just one element of the Balkan feuds. Scores had been robbed of their savings, Greek children had been kidnapped and held for ransom (some who were never returned to their parents), and many hundreds were forced into paying tribute to the Macedonians. It was even reported that in England, France, Germany, Italy, Spain and Russia there existed another 150 unsolved murdered cases of Macedonians, Bulgarians and Greeks likely attributable to IMRO or its 'Black Hand' spawn.[61]

These and other crimes, however, did not produce concrete evidence against Roumaneff and the Macedonians in Granite City. Still, for several months, Greek consuls in the U.S. had been accumulating evidence against them. They held Roumaneff's secret society responsible for nearly all unsolved murders where the victim was Greek, Bulgarian or Macedonian. They also had gathered testimonials about the Macedonians' operations in southwestern Illinois and St. Louis.

In November of 1906, one month prior to Roumaneff's arrest, the Greek officials publicly charged that the Macedonians' secret organization was headquartered in Granite City and that they held meetings near the American Steel Foundry Company. From that meeting place, said the Greeks, plans were hatched to force Greeks to pay money in exchange for peace. They accused the Macedonians of acting as a "junta" for IMRO in Macedonia. One Greek, on the condition of anonymity, relayed his knowledge to the press:

We have told the Consul all about it, and none of us cares to have his name used. It is a deep, dark, dangerous business. We know that there is a secret organization in Granite City. It has harassed us so much that we have selected A. D. Papas of 118 South Sixth Street as our representative to treat with the society. Mr. Papas has been going over there every day, but nothing we can do seems to satisfy them.

They always want more money. They tell us that if we do not pay them our people in Greece will be slaughtered by Macedonian raiders, who will rush across the border and kill our fathers and mothers and brothers and burn our towns. They say that the Turkish government is behind them. Of course, they make it appear that if we pay the money the raids will not take place. But we do not believe that. We are sure that they mean to use our money to buy arms with which to kill our people.

They have agents out collecting from the St. Louis Greeks and they are working in East St. Louis and Belleville, too. Sometimes they make open threats. They say to us: 'You have attacked our people and have caused them much loss. Now you have better jobs than we have in this country and you must help to support us.' Also they sometimes go to Greeks who are wanted at home for something they have done there and they say: 'Pay us or we will tell on you and you will be sent back.'[62]

The Macedonians, on the other hand, insisted that they were merely raising funds to ensure peace in Macedonia. The money was being sent to aid in education, libraries and other peaceful activities, they said, so their families could keep their minds off fighting their Greek neighbors.[63] That rebuttal, however, was not widely accepted.

Roumaneff was aware that the authorities and public had been alerted to the Macedonians' activities. Yet, he must have viewed the inconvenience merely as a hiccup and proceeded to take care of some business in Terre Haute, Indiana, on Illinois' eastern border, in early December. This would soon prove to be a mistake. Just a few weeks before his arrival, two Macedonians in Terre Haute, Thomas Temeton and Theodore Demos, were arrested for levying blackmail on Greeks, Bulgarians and Macedonians in the area. The immigrants lived in fear of the Macedonians and one report showed that nearly two dozen Bulgarians were found "huddled in close quarters, where they were living like animals, and were afraid to go about because of threats."[64] A friend therefore dispatched a letter to Roumaneff warning him that he would likely be arrested in Indiana because of these recent incidents and due to his suspected leadership role. He urged Roumaneff to return to Granite City and avoid detection.[65] Roumaneff was late in heeding his friend's advice.

What happened next is unclear, as different newspapers and court testimonies give different version of the events. One Greek, named Dimitri (Mike) Demetrios, said that Roumaneff and another Macedonian by the name of Cortif (Kortef) had approached him and demanded he pay them $3,000. He said they ordered him to pay $170 immediately and then $70 per month until the $3,000 was paid. If not, then they would kill him and send word to Macedonia to have his family tortured to death. Demetrios went to Belleville, Illinois (just 20 miles southeast of Granite City) to obtain the money but failed in securing enough. The Macedonians, who had followed him there, again threatened to kill him.[66]

In another telling of the tale, Demetrios and another Greek, Charles Evans (both from Macedonia) had been approached by Roumaneff in a similar fashion. They replied that they would immediately get him the money. Instead, they visited Captain Bray, a detective based in Indianapolis.[67] They told him that if they could not pay, their relatives in Macedonia "would be maimed, tortured and roasted like pigs."[68] Bray and his officers devised a scheme to catch the Macedonian mastermind. They marked certain bills in the amount of $50 for the Greeks to give as a down payment and instructed the Greeks to meet at the assigned location. Upon Roumaneff's arrival, the Greeks handed over the money, and then Roumaneff pocketed it after a quick count. Just moments after pocketing the cash, however, three detectives barged into the room. They searched Roumaneff, found the marked bills in his pockets, and placed him under arrest. Other Macedonians associated with Roumaneff were arrested as well and held for loitering until the police could muster up charges that could stick.[69]

The alleged victims described in detail how Roumaneff extracted money from them. A journalist reconstructed their story:

**'You must pay the equivalent of five pounds in Turkish money or – swish!' With the 'swish' went a gurgle, two uplifted shoulders and a significant gesture – a hand drawn swiftly across the 'swisher's' throat. The intimation was an open one. The two young Macedonians[70] understood it perfectly, and with staring eyes and cleaving tongues made bold to tremble... 'Have it ready when I call again or a branch of the society in Macedonia will be instructed to –**

**swish – your parents.' Again, the horrid gesture and the [victims] understood. With another growl of warning the black mustache was gone.**[71]

This was the Greek version of events, though. The suspects insisted on their innocence from the very beginning. At their arraignment, both Macedonians "admitted their connection with a secret society which [was] responsible for most of the internal disturbances" in Turkey during the past few years. Roumaneff even boasted that the society had been responsible for the assassination of Serbia's Queen Draga.[72] Roumaneff also admitted that there may be IMRO agents in America, but that neither he nor his friend were involved in any business that they might be conducting in America. He insisted that the society's purpose was for "the overthrowing of the Grecian and Turkish governments" and the establishment of an independent Macedonia governed by the Macedonian people.[73]

Roumaneff maintained his innocence, but the drama had just begun. For several months, he and his compatriots, Cortif and two Macedonian brothers named James and Stergius Vassily, would face off against the Greeks in the courtroom. Macedonians in Granite City, however, refused to abandon their 'Black Hand' duties. Shortly after Roumaneff's arrest, one of them mailed a letter to Demetrios instructing him to meet them at Market and Eight streets in St. Louis for a friendly rendezvous. Money was included for travel expenses. Demetrios found this strange and informed the police. The police sent a decoy instead; they suspected the Macedonians had no idea what Demetrios looked like. The police scheme was partly successful, as a number of Macedonians were detained for loitering near the scene of where the rendezvous was supposed to occur. Three Greek consuls then met in Chicago and issued a statement promising continued cooperation with the police and further reprisals if Macedonians persisted in making moves to revenge the incarceration of Roumaneff. Their attention would center on those Macedonians living in Granite City who were ordering Macedonians to murder other Balkan immigrants across the country.[74] Vice-consul Tsolomiti went as far as to say that the 'Black Hand' was seeking to levy blackmail on 100,000 Greeks, Bulgarians and Macedonians in America.[75]

The investigation into this Macedonian 'Black Hand' had now extended into Indianapolis, where there were allegedly scores of victims. The Greek consuls insisted the goal was for the Macedonian Committee in Sofia[76] to wrest Macedonia from the Turks, and that while crimes were committed nationwide, the 'Black Hand's' headquarters in America was Granite City.[77] But the Macedonians of Granite City had another version of events to relay to the courts; or rather, a few versions of events.

Dr. S. J. Shoomkoff, editor of a Macedonian newspaper in Granite City and graduate of the University of Chicago and University of Pennsylvania, insisted that the Greek consuls' assertions were nothing but creative manipulations of the facts. The truth, he said, was that the Greeks had created an elaborate revenge scheme against the Macedonians. He explained:

**Roumaneff[78] was active in a strike of Bulgarians and Macedonians at Granite City, Illinois, last summer. The Greeks took the places of the strikers, but their work was found to be unsatisfactory and the Macedonians and Bulgarians were returned to their jobs at an advance over what they had received before the strike. The Greeks swore vengeance, and seven days after Roumaneff came to Indianapolis he was arrested at the instance of the Greek persecuting committee, which sent a**

messenger here to inform the local committee of the order that he was in the city.

As to the Vassily brothers, one of them a mere boy, a Greek tried to compel them to pay him $2 every pay day in order to hold their jobs as laborers with the Vandalia Railroad Company. Other Macedonians were forced to pay the same amount, but the Vassilys refused. The foreman of the gang heard of the extortion and discharged the Greek. The charge of conspiracy against the Vassilys was trumped up as revenge for the discharge of the Greeks, and because the Macedonians would not pay the money demanded of them.

Unfortunately for the Greeks, they did not figure that Macedonians who are American citizens would become interested in the cases, and come to the aid of the Bulgarians and the Macedonians. We are ready for the continuance of the trial and have the evidence to prove that our men are innocent and that it is the Greeks who are blackmailing. They extort money from our people with threats and our men are entirely innocent of any crime.⁷⁹

That was one explanation, and eventually a compelling one for the judge in the case. Another defense asserted that all of accusations were a lie. Demetrios, said the defense, was a baker who had become enraged because Macedonians were boycotting his prices. They insisted he was not even a Greek but a Macedonian; he was a subject of Turkey like the rest of them and "the prosecution [was] making a mountain of a molehill."⁸⁰

These defenses, however, did not explain why Roumaneff was caught by detectives accepting marked bills. The Greeks insisted this was proof that extortion had taken place. The Macedonians, however, insisted that the conversation between the Greeks and Roumaneff was not in English, and so how could the detectives know for sure that the exchange of money was related to extortion?

This point was cleverly pointed out in a letter to the police and the press. It further detailed why Roumaneff was accepting money from Demetrios. The supporter (who remained anonymous) sent the letter to the *Indianapolis Star* in January of 1907. He clamored that Roumaneff's arrest was "one of the most unwarranted offenses against personal liberty." He accused a Greek by the name of Chimbouris, who was a timekeeper for a construction crew, for extorting two dollars each month from ignorant foreigners so they could keep their jobs. Roumaneff and a few other Macedonians, he said, refused to pay this tribute. Thus, the Greeks contrived a revenge plot against them. The concept of a Macedonian 'Black Hand' was created in the minds of Greeks, he said, so that the Greek leaders could continue terrorizing foreign workmen into paying them money for jobs and protection. He then elaborated on the details of Roumaneff's arrest:

**Chimbouris and Satiry set a trap for Roumaneff[81] and he fell in. Satiry met Roumaneff in a West Washington street saloon and asked if he spoke English. Roumaneff answered that he spoke it a little. Then Satiry asked him to go with him to the office of the Vandalia Railroad to draw his pay, as he wished to send some money home. They went to a room and met Chimbouris, who asked what they wanted. Satiry answered that he wished his pay as he had been working about thirty days and his home folks in Macedonia needed money, and that Roumaneff was to go with him to the post office to send the money. Chimbouris produced $50, saying that he had no bank of the company with him, but that Satiry could have the $50 if he would give the money to Roumaneff to carry to the post office, as he was afraid Satiry, who was drinking, would spend it.**

**After they were outside, Roumaneff offered him the money, but Satiry refused to take it, and told Roumaneff to send it to Macedonia. They went in a saloon to get a drink and were arrested by two officers, who had Chimbouris and another Greek with them. They searched Roumaneff and, of course, took away the money which Chimbouris claimed he had paid to Satiry. Roumaneff was a victim of circumstantial evidence, and nothing could clear him but his enemies, the Greeks.**[82]

While that letter was anonymously written, another prominent Macedonian, Basil Stephanoff, a preacher and activist, came to the public defense of the Macedonians. He set out to disprove the charges, along with Shoomkoff, and hinged his defense of the two by claiming that the Macedonian 'Black Hand' was in the mind of the Greeks. He said that the "Macedonians who come to this country come here to escape the tortures that are imposed upon them by the Turkish and Greek brigands. The Greeks for centuries have been trying to subjugate the Macedonians and the Bulgarians in Macedonia, and all kinds of tortures have been tried to further their aim."[83] Stephanoff spent several months during 1907 defending the Macedonian suspects. He visited Macedonian communities across the country to raise money for attorneys and court expenses. Stephanoff's and Shoomkoff's devotion to the case proved fruitful: the judge eventually shared their views that the Greeks here had conspired the whole case against the Macedonians for revenge.[84]

The road to acquittal, however, was not smooth. In March of 1907, D. Jannopia, Greek vice-consul in St. Louis, traveled to Indiana to participate in the case against the Macedonians.

Here, he and Stephanoff engaged in out-of-place and heated debates. Even the interpreters constantly disagreed and argued with one another. One interpreter was James Johnson, a Bulgarian banker in Indianapolis brought to the city by the accusers after they were unable to secure a Greek interpreter. Shoomkoff served as the Macedonians' interpreter and was constantly interrupting and correcting the interpretations of Johnson. One of the accusers said that he could speak better Greek than Bulgarian, and there was a roar in the courtroom when he said he was a Greek and not a Macedonian. The court then decided that the examination should proceed in Greek. But Shoomkoff "offered vigorous objections." "I do not speak Greek," he said, "and cannot check the court interpreter if the questioning is done in that language." The court then ordered the case to proceed in the Slavic tongue.[85] During some points of the trial, three interpreters were utilized because "knowledge of half a dozen Greek, Bulgarian and Macedonian dialects was required."[86] This certainly made it difficult for the judge to follow along.

Initially, Roumaneff was found guilty in a preliminary hearing at City Court. The court determined that he had been threatening Greek merchants for refusing to contribute to the revolutionary society. He also was suspected of ordering Macedonians and Bulgarians to boycott Demetrios' bakery because he refused to give money to Granite City's Macedonian 'Black Hand'.[87] However, that was overturned and a retrial was required. Moreover, the Macedonians were released on a $200 bond. The prosecution, however, insisted that this amount was too small and that Roumaneff would flee the country.[88] He did not flee, however, and in March of 1907, Roumaneff was found guilty and sentenced up to five years in prison under an indeterminate sentence law.[89]

On Roumaneff's conviction, it was stated that it was "the first time the laws in this country [had] been made effective against what Greeks [said was] a widespread conspiracy to levy tribute." A Macedonian witness even stated that Roumaneff had "asked him in Pittsburg to join him in levying this blackmail and said that with a few assassinations as a warning, Macedonians would pay promptly." Other witnesses testified that "the victim is told the names of kinsfolk in Macedonia and it is pointed out to him that word can be sent to the conspirators in Macedonia to destroy property or take the lives of kinfolk."[90] They freely talked to the press upon conviction perhaps because they felt threats to their lives would now be mitigated with Roumaneff in prison.

The case, however, saw more appeals. By July of 1907, after extensive involvement from Stephanoff, Shoomkoff and American attorneys, Roumaneff and the other Macedonians were freed.[91] The judge deemed the Greeks' version of events to be unbelievable. Thus, the 'Gospodar' escaped imprisonment and returned to his kingdom in Granite City.

While the specifics of this case went undetermined and a lack of credible evidence against the Macedonians secured them their freedom, blackmailing and racketeering escalated in Granite City and St. Louis in 1907. Reasonable estimates put the community of Macedonians and Bulgarians and Greeks (mostly from Macedonia) in Granite City and St. Louis during this time at about 8,000. Moreover, it was estimated that about one-fifth of all Macedonians in America were located in Granite City and its surroundings. The year of 1907 saw an increased in attempted assassinations, bar fights, and riots between the three ethnic groups, mostly between the Macedonians and the Greeks. The hostilities were fueled by Balkan feuds, the 'Black Hand' accusations, and the incarceration and then release of Roumaneff.[92]

The conflicts were abundant. For example, there were attempted assassinations against John C. Palmaris, an editor of a Greek newspaper in Chicago; C. N. Lanaris, an employment agency operator; and Basilius Georgopoulos, another Greek editor from East St. Louis. There was a failed attempt to smuggle weapons into Granite City after a suitcase of dynamite in a trunk exploded at the St. Louis train station. Further, on August 9, a street brawl erupted between Greeks and Macedonians in Hungary Hollow.[93]

Palmaris was targeted because he had written articles blasting Macedonians and Bulgarians for their extortion practices.[94] Many described the weekly he edited, called *Athena*, as merely a mouthpiece for anti-Macedonian and anti-Bulgarian propaganda. Palmaris said that this assassination attempt was due to the 'Black Hand's' hatred for his views.[95] He claimed he received a letter that stated he would be killed if he did not stop criticizing the Macedonians and Bulgarians.[96] He said:

**The Bulgarians[97] have a 'Black Hand' society, just as the Italians have. The letter I received was doubtless written by a member of that society in Granite City, where [they] are 7,000 strong. The society is called the Kommitazis [Komitas, IMRO]. The letter to me was written January 5, last, but I took no notice of it at that time, except by an article in the *Athena*, defying the author to attempt to harm me or to fight me in the open.[98]**

Palmaris also noted that some of the problems unfolding in Granite City were due to the fact that many Slavic-speaking Macedonians were more sympathetic to the Greek Church than to the Bulgarian Church, and those sympathetic to the Bulgarian Church were targeting those aligned with the Greek Church.[99]

The assassination attempt on C. N. Lanaris, St. Louis labor agent, was more personal: he had sent many Macedonians to Wyoming to work in unsatisfactory conditions. They returned to Granite City furious and swore they would make him pay for purposely sending them to Wyoming and pocketing their money. So, in late June of 1907, as Lanaris and Georgopoulos waited at the train station, a man arose from a hiding spot in the weeds near the station, raised a rifle, and fired at the two men. A bullet struck Lanaris in the thigh and Georgopoulos escaped unscathed. The Greeks demanded justice against these Macedonian 'Black Hand' agents. In pursuit of that justice, they did not meet resistance from some of the leading Macedonian figures in the community. Nick Alabach, considered one of the two "kings" of the Macedonian colony in Granite City and owner of a saloon, dry goods store, restaurant, bank and steamship agency, offered a reward of $100 for the arrest and conviction of Lanaris' assailant. He even visited Lanaris at the hospital as a sign of good faith.[100] Eventually, five Macedonians were arrested for the attempted murder, and all had been suspected of belonging to the Macedonian 'Black Hand' in Granite City.[101] The shooting of Lanaris also coincided with Sarafov's stay in Granite City, and some suspected he had played a role in the assassination attempt.[102]

In another instance, a trunk owned by Ivan Demmitri had arrived by train at the St. Louis train station and Naum Kristo, a Macedonian baker in St. Louis, went to retrieve it. However, as he approached it, the trunk exploded, injuring two nearby baggagemen.[103] Kristo said a man he did not know summoned him to recover the trunk, but authorities believed he had placed the dynamite in the suitcase.[104] Kristo was thus jailed for the explosion. Greeks in Granite City feared that dynamite was intended for them, so they increased security on their homes and businesses and even obtained permits to carry revolvers. The Macedonians then held an urgent meeting, according to Greek spies, but could not discern what had been discussed. Police obtained no evidence against Kristo, so they eventually released him. Moreover, they could not locate the owner of the trunk, Demmitri.[105]

In early August, many Greek laborers from a local labor bureau in Granite City refused to work, exclaiming they feared for their lives from the Macedonians in the boarding houses who called them dogs and threated to "fix them in the night." They demanded protection from the Macedonians. A few days later, the Greeks' worries were shown to have some grounds. Festivities from a Greek birthday party in Hungary Hollow leaked into Alabach's saloon. Macedonians looked to this intrusion as a provocation and immediately set upon the Greeks, whom they greatly outnumbered, with billiard cues and weapons. The brawl migrated to the streets until the police arrived. They arrested many, but also questioned why Greeks would visit a bar frequented and owned by Macedonians when they claimed the Macedonians were out to get them.[106]

The details of that battle are as follows: At 11:30 p.m., Greeks celebrating the birthday party of John Parker entered Alabach's saloon. Alabach and the Macedonians resented the rowdy Greeks, who were acting arrogant and disrespectful. The Greeks "climbed on the bar of his saloon in their eagerness to fight," which instigated a severe beating from Alabach and the Macedonians. The Greeks fought back but were greatly outnumbered. When the fight ended, "James Simon was lying on the floor bleeding from cuts on the head and scalp, William Christ was covered with blood that was streaming from a wound in his face and his body was battered where he had been kicked, and William George had many contusions on his head and face."[107]

The other Greeks retreated from the saloon and decided to regroup. They went to A. D. Pappas' saloon, the Blue Goose, where the Greek colony dominated. The St. Louis Post-Dispatch wrote:

**Pappas rallied the Greeks and marched out to renew the fight. Numerous shots had been fired in the neighborhood and when the police arrived they found Pappas at the head of his forces, armed with a pistol. He told the police that ... he wanted to march to his rival's saloon and do some execution with his pistol. The police stopped the march and sent the wounded men to the hospital for treatment.**

The Greeks claimed that Alabach had started the fight when he jumped onto the bar, proclaiming "that no Greeks were wanted in Granite City." One of the injured Greeks, William Christ, died.[108]

Dr. N. Salopoulos, the Greek consul at Chicago, blamed these and other murders of Greeks in Cairo, Illinois and in Kentucky on this Macedonian 'Black Hand'. He insisted that Greeks in Granite City and St. Louis lived in constant fear of Macedonians and Bulgarians and were, as a result, forced out of the area. He claimed that only 40 out of 600 Greeks remained in Granite City.[109] Salopoulos also visited Cincinnati, Ohio and talked to the Greeks there about the murders and extortion of Greeks. He said he had been investigating the 'Black Hand' since 1905 and that there were three branches located in Granite City, New York City, and Cincinnati. Here, he brought up the recent killing of a Greek in Columbus, Ohio, which he was certain could be attributed to the Macedonians.[110]

The Macedonian 'Black Hand' also targeted wealthy Macedonians. Two of the wealthiest in Granite City, Prodron V. Gosheff and Miko Hadji Misheff, were threatened in early October. They each were sent letters demanding that they straightaway give the organization $500. Misheff, fearing for his life, immediately took the letter to the chief of police. Gosheff, on the other hand, spent more time musing over the conundrum and consulted with a former police chief and a private investigator.[111]

The letters essentially said the same thing, except that the telephone poles designated as the drop-off locations for the money were different. The letter to Misheff said, for example:

**Eh, Misho,**

**Listen now to what I have to say. God has given you wealth, but God has also permitted me to kill you or your children wherever I find you, if you do not comply with my demand and give us $500, if you**

**wish to live undisturbed in the enjoyment of your money. Now the money in question you are to place near the eighth telephone pole, as you commence to count them from the corner of Pacific avenue and Olive street east, on the south side of the street. Know by this letter that I do not repeat, that I will kill you all if you don't place the money under a brick at the eighth pole.**[112]

Gosheff was instead ordered to place his money at the tenth pole. The detectives working the case devised a scheme and advised him to do as requested. They followed him into Hungary Hollow on a Friday night, remaining hidden in the distance. When Gosheff approached the pole, he noticed two shadowy forms standing on a railway switch that crossed the street. The detectives, who were half a block behind, were slowly crawling to the men. As soon as Gosheff dropped his package, however, the men spotted the detectives and ran away without looking at the money. Gosheff called for them to take the money, but they kept on running. The police never made any inroads into the matter but suspected that the letters were written by Macedonian leaders in order to throw suspicion onto the Greeks.[113]

Still, the Greeks were the Macedonians' main target. In the winter of 1908, Nicholas Pappas received a threatening letter from the 'Black Hand'. He was a relatively wealthy Greek in the St. Louis area, involved in real estate and other lucrative business. The letter read, in part: "I know you love your life, and if you want to save it you will come to Second and Florida street Saturday night with $300. Don't notify the police for your own benefit." Pappas immediately went to the local U.S. immigration agent who advised him to go to the police. Pappas indeed went to the police, but decided not to enlist their help, thinking that he could unravel the mystery himself. He went to the drop-off location with Jim Chiflas, a Greek interpreter from the Immigration Office, and they waited there for two hours. A few men approached them and studied them inquisitively but said nothing and left. Pappas received more threats, but never attributed much significance to them.[114]

By now, however, U.S. federal officials had caught wind of the racketeering, murder and general state of fear and hate plaguing Granite City. They inserted themselves into the mess by proclaiming that many immigrants residing in Granite City were there illegally and their statuses needed to be evaluated. Thus, in late January of 1908, Alcibiades Seraphis, the General Traveling Inspector for the Immigration Bureau, left Washington, D.C. and arrived in Granite City. His visit excited and agitated the Macedonians, Greeks and Bulgarians because Seraphis was originally one of them. A Greek immigrant, he had started out as an interpreter at Ellis Island and eventually became head of the department. Seraphis had "a reputation for always getting the man he [went] after and convicting him." The Macedonian 'Black Hand' particularly dreaded this. Seraphis clearly stated that his intention was to root out the illegal members of the Macedonian IMRO. He thus brought a team with him that consisted of four Balkan men and one American.[115]

Furthermore, Seraphis was concerned about the manner that Macedonian leaders may have been exploiting Macedonians, Bulgarians and Greeks irrespective of the activities of the 'Black Hand'. Five years prior, the Macedonian 'kings' of Granite City were laborers earning $1.50 a day in the mills. By 1908, they each had a net worth ranging between

$100,000 and $200,000 (between $2.5 and $5 million in today's value), and owned several hotels, saloons, banks, grocery stores, and clothing shops. According to one article, these leaders had virtually enslaved over 6,000 Macedonians, Bulgarians and Greeks in Granite City, Madison, and Venice.[116]

Seraphis spent two months investigating the conditions in Granite City. He discovered that when an immigrant left Macedonia, an agent would sell him a ticket to America for $62. One ticket, however, only cost $38. But since most peasants did not have $38 to spend, the immigrant had to pay nearly double for the fare to America. Upon arriving in Granite City, he would immediately begin working to pay off the ticket. But that would not be his only financial obligation to the Macedonian 'kings'. The labor agents would place the immigrant in a boarding house. His food was on credit at the boarding house's grocery stores, and the same went for the clothes he acquired from the clothing stores, as well as for the drinks ordered at the saloons. His check was delivered straight to an agent of the committee, who in turn gave him an account book in which his checks were entered on the credit side and purchases on the other side. In this manner, the books were often altered, and in this manner a Macedonian peasant would find himself in perpetual debt (not unlike his former life in Macedonia, where exorbitant taxes placed him in debt to the Turkish overlords). Furthermore, many immigrants were called on to contribute to the revolutionary fund; and if he demanded any of his money, the bosses threatened the lives of his relatives in Macedonia. Finally, these Macedonian leaders were accused of blocking the Macedonians' Americanization: they were given no opportunity to learn English and were taught that Americans were the enemy.¹¹⁷ The bosses themselves, however, were quite cozy with the Americans, including their language, politics and businesses.

With this investigation came an end to the Macedonian 'Black Hand' in Granite City. While not many arrests were made, some Macedonians and other immigrants were deported. It is unknown what happened to Roumaneff. Perhaps he was deported, perhaps he fled. Seraphis' arrival had also coincided with an economic downturn that affected Granite City's factories and therefore the Macedonian laborers, causing many to disperse from the city. Within a year, the population had been halved.

The Macedonian population would again grow – and it would come back strong – and this was in part due to Macedonian colony's leaders. These "Kings of the Macedonian Colony" avoided a crackdown and any serious trouble, and they continued to expand their dominions for several years. But kings are always rising and falling.

# THREE
# Kings of the Colony

The Macedonians who settled in Granite City mostly settled in the southwestern part of the city, known as Hungary Hollow. Many Macedonians coming to America had little choice in their destination; their travel, living arrangements, and employer were practically lined up for them once they secured a ticket. The first financially successful Macedonians in America were located in Illinois and these leaders had established cozy operations that stretched from the villages of Macedonia to the streets of Hungary Hollow. Some of the wealthiest and notable Macedonians in Granite City of that time include Nick Alabach, Karl (Kosta) Mitsareff, Misho Mitseff, the Gitcho Brothers, Prodron Gosheff, Evangelov, and Lazaroff. Although outsiders looked to them as opportunists and overlords, their own Macedonians viewed them as spokesmen and providers.[118]

Christ N. Gitcho was one of these first Macedonians in Granite City. Born in Smrdesh, just outside of Kostur, Macedonia[119] in 1877, Gitcho arrived in America in 1902. He first lived in New Bedford, Massachusetts and then Dayton, Ohio before moving to St. Louis around 1903. In 1904, he started a small business in Venice, which was just south of Madison. His business flourished and in 1905, he and his brothers began construction of a four-story building in Madison, bordering on Granite City. The building was completed in 1906 and from there he operated a grocery store, a general merchandise store, and a banking business. Christ owned and operated those stores (or variants of them) for nearly three decades and closed shop in 1931.[120] The Gitcho brothers (known as the *Gichevi*) boasted the first and oldest Macedonian-owned shopping center in America, which included a bakery, meat shop, and saloon. They also had an agency that sent money to Bulgaria and Macedonia.[121]

Like the Gitcho brothers, nearly all the wealthy Macedonians in the region operated saloons and boarding houses, such as Lazaroff, Evangelov, Mitsareff and Alabach. The latter two, however, were the true rulers of the Macedonian colony in Granite City; and it is through studying their mini-empires we can truly gain appreciation for the magnitude of their wealth and power. While all the aforementioned men were fantastically wealthy, especially given their humble peasant beginnings, only Alabach and Mitsareff were regarded as "Kings of the Macedonian Colony."

Nick Alabach, also spelled Alaback, was born in Brusnik, Macedonia, just three miles west of Bitola. The Macedonian iteration of his name was Nikola Alabakov, but he Americanized it upon his entry into America.[122] According to his World War I Draft Registration Card, he was born on December 8, 1877. That same document listed his nationality as Macedonian.[123] He married Vasilika (Vasa), who was about his same age, in Brusnik, and there they had a son named Jovan (John). However, Alabach soon developed an itch to find his fortune in America. He arrived in the U.S. in 1903 and found his way to the factories of Granite City. As the factories grew and demanded cheap labor, Alabach devised business plans to draw hundreds of Macedonians to Granite City. These business operations took off quickly, and his wife and son joined him in

1906. He and Vasa would eventually have three more daughters: Olga, Todora, and Elena.[124]

Alabach's accumulation of wealth, power and respect in Granite City deserve special attention. He spent just over a year working in the factories of Granite City before he devised a strategy to make money off supplying Granite City's factory with cheap Macedonian laborers. This operation eventually helped grow the immigrant colony in Hungary Hollow, and Alabach's located his headquarters at Pacific Avenue and Olive Street. The primary operations included a saloon, hotel, boarding house, restaurant, and bank.[125]

His complex was such an integral aspect of Granite City and the surrounding areas that it was often referred to as the Alabach Building by locals, Macedonians and Americans alike. For example, in 1909, B. Pencoff put an advertisement in a newspaper looking for a blacksmith job and indicated that he lived in the Alabach Building.[126] Another individual placed an advertisement in the newspaper for a hospital position and also listed his address as the Alabach Building.[127] The complex had several boarding rooms and several of the boarders touted the name with pride, as Alabach was respected by many in the area. In 1920, even when the number of Macedonians in Granite City had fallen quite drastically, he still had 34 boarders living there: 22 were Macedonians (of which one was from Albania); five were Armenians; four were Mexicans; and three were Bulgarians.[128] The boarding house was a substantial source of extra income for Alabach.

Like the other wealthy Macedonians in Granite City, Alabach provided clothing, food, drinks and banking services for the Macedonians, especially those that lived in his boarding house. While this was convenient for many Macedonians who found it easier to deal with their own people in their own tongue, there was occasionally friction. Nearly everything was based off credit and Alabach would deduct his tenants' dues from their paychecks at the end of the week. While investigations showed that some of these wealthy Macedonians were taking advantage of their boarders, this was not proven in Alabach's case. Sometimes, however, boarders would spend more than they earned, which left Alabach no choice but to withhold their paychecks.

This happened, for example, in June of 1908, with the Macedonian brothers Anton and Lepter Pulos. Alabach, who was referred to as "a prominent Macedonian merchant of Hungary Hollow," held up the brothers' pay in the steel mill for a debt that they owed to him. The brothers were enraged: they visited his store, threatened to kill him and blow up his building if he did not release their wages. Alabach remained calm and summoned the police. The brothers were then found and arrested by the police chief for threatening to kill Alabach. Without their pay, however, the brothers could not post bond and stayed in jail throughout their trial.[129]

Two other business operations that were vital to Alabach's success during his first decade in Granite City were his banking agency and weekly newspaper, *Macedonia*. Not only did this newspaper inform readers about Macedonian politics, but Alabach used it to promote his own businesses and discredit other businesses. For example, in May of 1908, with Shoomkoff as editor of *Macedonia*, the paper printed lengthy articles about the way Macedonians and Bulgarians had been "swindled by the [other] commercial houses of Granite City." An advertisement then followed that highlighted Alabach's banking agency in Granite City. It noted that Alabach was extending his operations to Indianapolis and other cities, including Toledo, Dayton, Pittsburg, Steelton, Chicago and Toronto – cities with large Macedonian communities. The advertisement highlighted that Alabach's bank had a fundamental capital of $50,000, or over $1.3 million dollars in today's value.[130]

The advertisement then made a final appeal for the Macedonians' business:

**We send money with checks to well-known banking institutions, also notes with best conditions for Macedonians. Your money is always warranted. We receive money for a year or less time. Those for one year deposits we pay 3 per cent interest. We give (or lend) money with lawful percentage for solid guarantee (or security). We exchange any kind of money. Our firm has twenty-one buildings, thirteen lots or places for building we rent. Our people [living with] us will find rooms furnished at reasonable prices. To all we show a brotherly welcome.[131]**

Indeed, Alabach's business did grow as the other large Macedonian banker in town, Mitsareff, slowly watched his life's work disappear. Moreover, it was the slogan and practice of embracing 'brotherly spirit' that kept Alabach afloat.

However, the scathing attacks on other Macedonians by Alabach's *Macedonia*, with Shoomkoff at its helm, found them at odds with the rival newspaper in Granite City, *Naroden Glas*. For several months, the men behind the press engaged in written and verbal arguments, and sometimes even physical confrontation. By August of 1909, this feud between Alabach and T. Evanoff, a writer for the *Naroden Glas*, was sent to the courts. Throughout the entire year, Granite City witnessed several fights between Alabach supporters and Evanoff and his crew. On August 1, for example, Evanoff entered Alabach's coffee house in Hungry Hollow uninvited. Mike Jim, Kote Moniroff, and Alabach were suspicious of Evanoff's presence, who began snooping around without ordering anything. He proceeded to antagonize Alabach and his patrons and a fight then ensued. Evanoff denied this rendering of the events, but he was still fined because the judge said he should have known better and stayed away from Alabach's place. Evanoff, however, appealed to the County Court. The judge reversed the lower court's decision and Alabach was fined three dollars for disturbing the peace. Alabach refused to pursue the case further and handed over the pocket change.[132]

Prior to this event, Alabach's editor, Shoomkoff, took the editor of *Naroden Glas*, Christo Nedelkoff, to court. The dispute, which seemed trivial, was just part of an ongoing battle between the different factions in town. Shoomkoff had instituted criminal libel charges against Nedelkoff for attacks against him in a newspaper that Shoomkoff described as malicious libel.[133] The jury found Nedelkoff guilty and fined him $25 and court costs of $150. Nedelkoff's article insinuated that the shoes Shoomkoff wore at a speech were not his, suggesting that he had stolen them.[134]

Alabach had a command over hundreds of Macedonians, and many more immigrants. They respected him and thus listened to him when he spoke on a variety of issues. One topic he tried to educate Macedonians about was public health. The Macedonians had come from 'country living' in Macedonia to more crowded and communal living in American cities. Thus, Alabach began encouraging Macedonians to bathe more often. He instituted a ritual where all Macedonians under his sway would take a monthly dip in the waters at "Gabaret Slough," two miles southwest of Granite City. It was something Alabach also touted as a small step toward the Americanization of the Macedonians.

However, during one of these monthly plunges in the summer of 1910, tragedy befell the plungers. Nearly 750 Macedonians had ventured to the shores on July 24, as directed by Alabach. After a brief speech and ceremony, "King Alabach" (as the newspaper wrote) commanded the Macedonians to enter the water. Anthony Stefoff, who was 28 years old, had never participated before. Like all first-timers, he was nervous and thus remained close to shore. Suddenly, though, he fell face downward into two feet of water. His fellow Macedonians ignored him for a while because they thought that he was playing and that he would get back up on his own. But after a few moments of a motionless Stefoff, they realized he had died. Many men were shocked that a man could drown in two feet of water, which made Macedonians even more nervous about participating in the bathing ritual. As the undertaker's wagon transferred Stefoff's body to the coroner's office, hundreds of Macedonians followed behind. Like many of the Macedonians there, Stefoff was single and lived in one of Alabach's boarding houses.[135]

Putting aside this tragic incident, Alabach's desire to promote the Americanization of his fellow Macedonians was indeed sincere. Perhaps he figured that it would be more profitable for him, or perhaps he envisioned establishing a permanent colony in Granite City of Macedonian-Americans: perhaps both reasons factored into his attempt to Americanize the Macedonians. Regardless, he devised ambitious plans for the Americanization of the Macedonians and other immigrant communities in Granite City.

In March of 1915, Alabach led a group of wealthy foreigners in creating plans to establish a capital for the over 2,000 foreigners remaining in Granite City, Madison and Venice. The capital was to include a large building with assembly halls, a gymnasium, libraries of books from the many nations represented in Granite City, and other facilities that would be beneficial and useful to the newcomers' integration into society. Until 1915, the foreign melting pot was located at the Bulgarian Orthodox Church in Hungry Hollow, which included "Macedonians, Poles, Armenians, Servians, Greeks, Slavs, Hungarians, Bohemians and Bulgarians." Alabach desired a headquarters "where foreigners [would] gather for mutual education and spiritual benefit and recreation and absorb the principles of Americanism."[136]

This proposal did not unfold in the manner which the foreigners anticipated. However, Alabach turned this proposal into another plan: the rebranding of Hungary Hollow. On March 19, 1916, the name of Hungary Hollow was officially changed to Lincoln Place in honor of President Abraham Lincoln.[137] This change was initiated by Alabach and other immigrant community leaders of the Lincoln Progressive Club. Hungary Hollow had a negative association in the surrounding American community and the immigrant leaders wanted to change their perception.[138] Alabach presided over the meeting as chairman; Lincoln Place's new bylaws were explained in several languages and then adopted by a unanimous vote. The Board of Governors included other Macedonians, such as Vassil Stephanoff and Mike Rousseff, who was elected president.[139]

In just over a decade, Alabach transformed Granite City in ways unlike any other Macedonian. He brought hundreds of Macedonians to work in the factories, providing a beneficial relationship for him and the factories; he built boarding houses, opened shops, and started a banking agency, which helped immigrants smoothly transition into life in America; and he supported both the Macedonian identity and the Americanization of Macedonians through his newspaper, elaborate community projects and well-attended events.

Another "king" in the Macedonian Colony, however, took a different approach to the Macedonian community. Kosta (Karl) Mitsareff, also known as Charley Anastas, arrived in America in 1900, a few years prior to Alabach's arrival. Mitsareff was born in Macedonia in 1874 to parents Anastas Mitsareff and Yota Mitsir.[140] He had a few brothers –who would eventually join him in the U.S. – but Kosta Mitsareff was the first of his family to come here and was among the first Macedonians to settle in Granite City.

While Alabach grew his wealth and dominion in Hungary Hollow in just a few short years, Mitsareff is honored with essentially igniting that section of Granite City as a Macedonian sanctuary. Although Hungary Hollow derived its name from the first few Hungarian immigrants that settled in that part of Granite City during the early 1900s, it quickly became dominated by Macedonians. By 1906 it was described as "a colony of 1,000 Macedonian men with no women." Mitsareff even blessed the colony with a new name by the end of 1906:

New Macedonia. The name was only ever used unofficially during that period, but it was widely enough accepted for newspapers to utilize the terminology.[141] So, how did Mitsareff help grow this New Macedonia?

When Mitsareff arrived in America in 1900, he had just enough money to get him from New York City to St. Louis. He started working in the Niedringhaus brothers' foundry. After a while, he made an impression on the brothers and became acquainted with them. He told them, like Alabach told others, that he could get hundreds of Macedonians from his homeland to come work here. In this way they helped each other out: the Niedringhaus brothers said they would accept the cheap Macedonian laborers and in exchange would help Mitsareff establish the amenities and operations to board and serve them. This mutual relationship between Mitsareff and the Niedringhaus brothers lasted for several years. For example, in 1908, Mitsareff placed an advertisement in a newspaper claiming that one of their grandsons cured him of typhoid fever:

**I herewith publicly acknowledge my gratitude toward Dr. R. N. Niedringhaus, one of the medical staff of the Granite City Hospital, for the personal interest and care in my protracted illness of typhoid fever, and his ability to successfully combat all complications arising therefrom. I was in the grip of typhoid fever and death, but his skill saved my life, and helped me to regain my former vigor and strength.[142]**

By the end of 1906, Mitsareff was in possession of three buildings and several lots in Granite City. On these lots he eventually built several rows of boarding houses. During this time, the Macedonian community respected and adored him. Mitsareff knew that if he looked out for the Macedonians, then they would be more likely to come to him for their needs. "If one of the Macedonians gets into trouble," said one article, "[then] the king will make an investigation if he believes it is his duty to do so. If his subject is found to be to blame, the king will make no effort to interfere, but if the trouble should be with the civil authorities and the Macedonian's rights are at stake, then the king will aid him." Mitsareff did possess the means to assist the Macedonians. In addition to his friendship with the Niedringhaus family, he was close to many other prominent men in the city. One such of these men was A. W. Morris, a realty broker in Granite City. The two had become so close in financial business and transactions that Morris donated a large parcel of land to the Macedonians so that they had a place to conduct Orthodox religious services on Sundays. Morris even offered to help them raise funds for construction of the church beginning in 1907.[143]

Mitsareff owned land and operated boarding houses, like many of the other wealthy Macedonians. He was especially known, however, for his steamship agency and banking institution. The latter two were responsible for his accumulation of $500,000 in wealth by the beginning of 1908.[144] To put that in perspective, Mitsareff went from empty pockets to a net worth of over $13 million in today's value in just eight years. That kind of wealth accumulation was not only unprecedented for an immigrant from a village in Macedonia, but it was rarely heard of in America at that time.

In 1907, Mitsareff and other bankers (like Alabach, Misheff, Evangelov, and Lazaroff) expanded their operations to other

Macedonian colonies in America. Mitsareff was the first to penetrate the Indianapolis market. This venture was successful, for a short time. Others saw him take his business to the Macedonians there and followed suit. However, unlike Alabach, these bankers skirted banking laws and ethics and soon found themselves persecuted by state officials and auditors.

For example, in 1908, R. B. Oglesbee of the Indiana State Auditor's office, declared that some of the biggest banks in Illinois were Macedonian-owned. Oglesbee had been keeping an eye on Mitsareff's bank, which he called "the wild cat" bank, and this led him to initiate investigations into the practices of other Macedonian bankers in Granite City. He hired an interpreter (Basil Stephanoff) and scoured the pages of the Macedonian newspapers published in Granite City and Michigan to better understand these banks' breadths and practices.[145]

He discovered, firstly, that the different banks were engulfed in a propaganda war as they competed for territory. Some of the articles particularly attacked Mitsareff for deceit:

**The A. Balkanic Association [Mitsareff's bank] has claimed that they have deposits as fundamental capital of $10,000, when in fact have not a cent. ... It is said they represent the banking house and the steamship company but Mitsareff of late has opened a branch in Indianapolis according to the words of Mitsareff. Mitsareff, the famous banks in Granite City and Indianapolis, owe to the American Balkanic Association $5,000, to the others $1,000.[146]**

Another article in May of 1908 proclaimed:

> Uncontroverted fact is that the American company, the United States Express Company, has commanded to ... Mitsareff ... not to issue [his] checks in sending money to Europe, because about ten checks have been returned from Paris because the needful credit, or better say the money, were not sent to the United States Express Company, but our bankers, so to say, continue to practice against the laws and deceive ... with green of piece of paper (checks), which are not worth a pipeful of tobacco.[147]

The State of Indiana, in conjunction with Illinois officials, opened an investigation into Mitsareff's bank to determine if he was illegally operating in Indiana. His bank in Indianapolis, which was on West Washington Street, had been operating for several months by that point. His two agents in the Indianapolis branch were Jordan Piperka and Michael Dosheff. State officials summoned Mitsareff to Indiana after not being able to acquire information from his agents, so Mitsareff arrived in Indianapolis in May of 1908. He refused to let the State Auditor examine his books and went back to Granite City to get bondsmen for Piperka and Dosheff, who had been jailed on charges of violating the private banking laws. Oglesbee, however, had a hard time collecting evidence against Mitsareff and his practices because the Macedonians who would gather in a saloon near the bank building refused to talk. "They fear a mysterious death if they talk too freely," he said.[148]

Mitsareff's problems started in 1907, when he decided to take a vacation from his business, do some traveling in America, and then visit his homeland. After seven years he had accumulated a massive fortune and finally felt that his financial situation was relatively secure. He owned a bank, steamer agency, saloon and labor agency, which gave him an endless stream of money: he was paid to bring Macedonians to America; he was paid to find them work; he was paid to house them; and he was paid to quench their thirst. Moreover, he was known as a "King of the Macedonian and Bulgarian Colony" in Granite City, and thus he had hundreds of immigrants who respected and depended on him. When he left Granite City for Florida and then Macedonia, he put his brother-in-law, Prodron Gosheff, in charge of his business affairs.[149] This decision, according to Mitsareff, was the ruin of his financial empire.

Gosheff's close involvement in Mitsareff's business operations was Mitsareff's own doing. After a few years in America, Mitsareff brought three of his brothers to Granite City and they won the confidence of their ethnic kin from Macedonia; first, because they helped bring them to America, and second, because they helped them find jobs. These Macedonian immigrants began depositing their earnings with the Mitsareff brothers; some of their deposits were sent to their families in Macedonia, and the rest was secured with someone they could trust. (Most Macedonians did not speak English and thus did not particularly trust Americans; moreover, it was dangerous to carry hundreds of dollars in their pockets, something for which the Macedonians had a notorious reputation.) With this capital, Mitsareff and his brothers expanded their grocery and saloon businesses, which built a big trade among the Macedonians in the area. Deposits increased and they became financial leaders of the colony, controlling many times more money than other Macedonians in the area.[150]

However, one of Mitsareff's brothers, Nicholas, was killed in America under suspicious circumstances. Nicholas, who was Mitsareff's main business partner, was shot and killed just outside of their grocery store and saloon. It was never ascertained who had killed him. Mitsareff insisted that robbery was the motive and that $500 had been taken from his brother's body. A few days later, Mitsareff said that two Macedonians turned over to him $500 that had been taken from the dead man, and he further said that the Macedonians claimed the money was given to them by African-American men that they could not identify. Granite City police at the time noted that there was "current rumor among the Macedonians" that the Turkish government had issued a reward of $10,000 for the Mitsareff brothers and that this might have had something to do with the murder. But the case went cold and no arrests were made.[151]

This was not the only tragedy to befall the Mitsareff brothers. In 1909, a gasoline explosion at one of Mitsareff's brother's houses badly injured his brother John and killed his other brother Mitri. It is unclear if John, who had served as an IMRO rebel, died that evening; but the explosion was suspicious, and in just a span of three years, at least two Mitsareff brothers were dead.[152]

With his brother Nicholas out of the picture, Mitsareff needed a new partner. His other brothers were not management material, so he therefore sent for the next logical choice: his sister's brother, Gosheff. The two had been friends in Macedonia and relatively successful: Mitsareff became a teacher and Gosheff worked as a clerk at his father's flour milling business. Eventually, Gosheff married Mitsareff's sister and they remained in Macedonia while Mitsareff pursued his fortune in America. After his brother died, Mitsareff sincerely believed that Gosheff would be capable of handling the work and that he would be able to trust him. Thus, in 1906, Gosheff made his way to Granite City.[153]

After a year of working together, Mitsareff felt he could trust Gosheff with all his business affairs. He left Gosheff in charge while he paid a visit to Macedonia. However, when Mitsareff returned in 1908, his financial empire had begun to disintegrate. A financial depression had hit Granite City and many Macedonians were jobless and fleeing the area. Mitsareff's bank failed and hundreds of Macedonians' deposits disappeared with it.[154]

Mitsareff held Gosheff directly responsible. So, in the summer of 1909, he had his brother-in-law arrested on the charge of stealing $35,000 from him through the bank they had operated together. Just prior to Mitsareff's charge against his brother-in-law, Mitsareff had filed a petition for voluntary bankruptcy. Gosheff then left Granite City and went to New York City, where he bought an interest in a successful restaurant. Mitsareff accused Gosheff of running away with his money. He tracked Gosheff to New York and had him placed under arrest.[155]

In particular, Mitsareff charged that while he was in Europe, Gosheff looted his bank, making away with several thousand dollars in other Macedonians' deposits and money obtained from banks and other institutions under Mitsareff's name. This caused the collapse of their bank, insisted Mitsareff. Gosheff, however, denied that he made away with any money. He claimed that when Mitsareff entered into bankruptcy, he figured that the best thing for himself was to get away from Granite City and start anew.[156]

Regardless, an application was made to the Illinois governor for requisition papers and an officer from Granite City went to New York City to bring Gosheff back to Granite City. Deputy Sheriff G. F. Crowe arrived back in Granite City with Gosheff in late June. Gosheff had been arrested in New York City two weeks prior due to the grand jury indictment of forgery. But Gosheff did not post bond and remained in county jail. He first obtained an attorney in New York City in order to fight the extradition; but they advised him not to fight his extraction to Illinois based on technicalities and to instead defend against the actual charges in Illinois.[157]

Gosheff denied the charges that he embezzled $30,000 worth of bank funds. Instead, he claimed that Mitsareff owed him $3,000 in unpaid wages. However, the receiver of the company had informed him that he could only file a claim for three months' salary. He loitered around Granite City following bankruptcy proceedings against Mitsareff but could not find work. That is when he left for New York, he said, where he secured a job at a restaurant. He saved up enough money and bought interest in the restaurant.[158] The charges and counter-claims between Mitsareff and Gosheff resulted in no convictions.[159]

Mitsareff's feud with his brother-in-law was just one of his many problems. In the spring of 1909, Mitsareff was arrested on charges of forgery and larceny. The forgery charge stemmed from a letter written to Macedonians and Bulgarians in West Virginia that was signed by G. Zapuroff, editor of the *Naroden Glas* at the time. Zapuroff insisted that he did not write the letter and that it had instead been written either by Mitsareff or Mitsareff's secretary. Regarding the larceny charge, many Macedonians claimed they had sent Mitsareff money in exchange for French *napoleons*. Many said they never received the *napoleons* owed to them. For example, Mitre Tarotoff, Atanas Elicoff, and Stoyan Tegoff, all of Ira, West Virginia, said they had been sent acknowledgement confirming their cash had been received and that *napoleons* would soon be sent. The confirmation letter from Mitsareff said that the men should immediately put their money in a specific bank in case they were delayed in making their trip to Macedonia. "You might become victims of theft or crime, remembering that we live in a sinful world," said the letter.[160]

Six months later, the men had not received their *napoleons*. They then sent a letter to Zapuroff asking him to investigate Mitsareff. Zapuroff claimed he never received the letter. He and Mitsareff received their mail in the same box, and it was alleged that Mitsareff found the letter addressed to the editor and opened it. Seeing that the letter accused him of larceny, he penned a reply using Zapuroff's name that highly praised himself and attested to his genius. Zapuroff denied that the handwriting was his.[161]

At his court case, Stoyan Tegoff and several other "Bulgarians and Macedonians" from West Virginia testified against Mitsareff. Mitsareff had only sent them $500 in *napoleons* for the $3,000 in U.S. cash that they had sent to him, they claimed. Mitsareff contended that he went to New York to get the *napoleons* but was forced into bankruptcy before he could get them. The letter that Mitsareff allegedly forged in Zapuroff's name stated that Zapuroff personally visited

Mitsareff's bank and Mitsareff showed him $20,000 in the safe. It went on to say that Mitsareff was ready to return the money, "but why should a company be made to lose when on the contrary their object is to gain?"[162]

The letter even boasted that Mitsareff was the richest and smartest Macedonian in Granite City. It further stated:

**I visited some American merchants who know [Mitsareff] well, on purpose, who told me that he had bought 28 rooming houses, and I know myself that he maintains two saloons, two groceries, one dry goods store, bakery, banks, and besides he has two large houses of forty years each and every day earn more than $300. And as proof of that, I can assure you that last year, when the people were starving on account of the crisis, he supported 600 hungry Bulgarians and Macedonians for fully six months. From all that we may derive the conclusion that Mr. Mitsareff is not the man who would wish to misappropriate other people's money.[163]**

The court could not conclusively prove that Mitsareff forged the letter and he was eventually acquitted of the charges.

Although Mitsareff avoided imprisonment, his financial situation only deteriorated. By 1911, he still harbored animosity toward his brother-in-law, who he claimed instigated his ruin. After returning to Granite City to face Mitsareff's accusations, Gosheff decided to remain there and rekindle his life with his wife, Mitsareff's sister. Even though their empire had failed for $1,000,000 (over $25 million in today's value) and Macedonians in Granite City lost hundreds of thousands of dollars, Gosheff came out relatively unscathed.[164]

After Mitsareff declared bankruptcy, A. W. Morris (the realtor and close business associate that donated the land to the Macedonians for an Orthodox church) assumed control

Mitsareff's properties. He turned the business over to a merchant who failed to turn a profit out of them, so Morris repossessed the businesses. Shortly thereafter, he turned the premises over to Gosheff in February of 1911. Mitsareff, meanwhile, had attempted several times to reclaim his property but was ignored by Morris. This infuriated Mitsareff, and his resentment against Gosheff and Morris grew deeper.[165]

When Mitsareff had left his operations in Gosheff's control in 1907, life was good. During his return-trip to Macedonia, he married his childhood sweetheart, Elena. He returned to America with his bride and sister, Gosheff's wife. But upon his return, he found that his business had been mismanaged and undermined. The financial depression hit Granite City and many men lost work. Piece-by-piece his properties had to be sold off; and by coincidence or conspiracy, Gosheff was always the purchaser. By 1911, Gosheff possessed all the grocery stores, saloons, bank and offices that had once belonged to Mitsareff. This included a pretentious office in a dressed stone building in Granite City's business district. Gosheff had bought the beautiful stone building on a mortgage foreclosure and planned to open his own store in it.[166]

All this resentment and anger gnawed away at Mitsareff's being. He watched his empire crumble and his brother-in-law collect the pieces for himself. On March 21, 1911, Mitsareff's friends observed that had been in a terrible mood the whole day. At a Macedonian saloon, he announced he would kill someone and that the victim would be A.W. Morris. His friends in Granite City did not attach importance to Mitsareff's threats, as he was constantly rambling on about his anger toward Gosheff and Morris. No one decided to warn Morris. Mitsareff believed that Morris had enabled Gosheff to get the better of him in real estate deals regarding his former properties. Morris had always insisted that this accusation was groundless.[167] The fact of the matter, however, is that on that first day of spring, a constable acting on Gosheff's behalf served Mitsareff an eviction notice to evacuate a building that Mitsareff was using as an office. Mitsareff protested, but Gosheff took control and Mitsareff was booted to the street.[168]

Four hours later, Mitsareff murdered Gosheff in the same spot where Mitsareff's brother had been robbed and murdered five years prior – the entrance to Gosheff's grocer and saloon, formerly owned by Mitsareff. Gosheff had left the store with his wife at 7:00 p.m. but went back to retrieve a quarter to pay for the gaslight which kept the store lit. As he stepped into the store, four shots were fired from across the street. The shots pierced his arm, thigh, and heart. Gosheff's wife, who was half a block away and saw the man come across the street, could not immediately identify him.[169]

An hour later, the police chief stormed Mitsareff's home. The house was unlit, so he entered with a revolver in one hand and a lantern in another. Upon entering, he found Mitsareff crouching behind a piano, with a revolver pointed at the door. "I've got the drop on you," said the police chief. "All right," replied Mitsareff. "I killed him. I don't care if you hang me. He caused my family enough trouble."[170]

At court, however, Mitsareff altered his story. He said he shot Gosheff at the door of the saloon only after Gosheff made a move as though to draw a revolver and threatened to kill him. "Then I got him first," said Mitsareff. Mitsareff's case, however, fell to shambles because no weapon was found on Gosheff's body.[171] Moreover, his sister, Mrs. Gosheff, testified in court against her brother. She now claimed that she saw Mitsareff shoot her husband without reason and in the cold-blood. She said she was absolutely sure that she saw her brother emerge from behind a telephone pole and shoot Gosheff.[172]

Mitsareff was convicted by the jury for first degree murder. In an ironic twist, the gun that Mitsareff used to kill Gosheff had actually been a Christmas gift from Gosheff to Mitsareff during Gosheff's first Christmas in America.[173] Mitsareff was sentenced to 14 years in prison but was paroled within just a few years.[174]

Shortly after his release, Mitsareff went to Morris' office in Granite City in February of 1918 to discuss a business disagreement. Mitsareff pulled a gun on Morris who then pulled out his own gun. The two men exchanged fire in Morris' office, but Morris got the better of the duel: he landed three bullets in Mitsareff's abdomen. Mitsareff ran out of the office straight for the National Bank of Granite City, shouting that he intended to "get" D. J. Murphy, a cashier at the bank. However, he dropped his gun on the street and lost consciousness when he reached the bank lobby. Mitsareff took his last breath on the floor of the bank lobby.[175]

Mitsareff's two decades in America can be defined as the epitome of success, failure and tragedy. He became the wealthiest Macedonian in America in just a few years. He owned and operated boarding houses, saloons, a labor agency, a steamship agency, a bank, a grocery store and a restaurant, in addition to many other business ventures. But in the same amount of time, he lost it all. His wealth disappeared; his brothers were dead; he killed his wife's husband; and he died in an attempt to avenge all those who he believed had wronged him. In under two decades he went from Macedonian serf to American king, to a disgraced convict who had nothing left to live for.

Mitsareff's story, however, was uncommon for both immigrants and Americans. Most Macedonians in Granite City, including the wealthy, led relatively peaceful and respectful livelihoods. All of these Macedonian kings, however, shared humble beginnings with their Macedonian compatriots. They, too, were once normal.

# PART II

# The New Normal

# FOUR
# The Daily Grind

Credible estimates of the Macedonian population in Granite City are hard to come by. Some estimates include all individuals from Macedonia (including ethnic Greeks) as Macedonians; other estimates count everyone speaking a Slavic dialect from Macedonia as Bulgarian. Moreover, the nature of the Macedonian immigrant experience was fluid: most Macedonians remained in Granite City or its environs only for a few years. These Macedonian men amassed a small fortune from long hours of arduous labor, and then returned to Macedonia to enjoy the fruit of their labor. Moreover, the rise and fall of industry in Granite City and the wild swings in the economy kept the Macedonian population constantly in flux.

One estimate suggests that the combined Macedonian and Bulgarian population of the Granite City area (including Macedonians in Madison and Venice) was 15,000 in 1910.[176] About four-fifths, or 12,000, of these likely would have been Macedonians. However, this figure is an exaggeration. The U.S. Census puts the populations of these three cities in 1910 at just under 20,000. Being that St. Louis had no more than 1,000 of these Macedonians at the time, it is a significant distortion to suggest that about two-thirds of the Tri-Cities' population consisted of Macedonians.

Still, it is likely that the area's Macedonian population consistently ranged between one-fourth and one-third of the area's total population between 1905 and 1915. Scores of boarding houses popped up in Granite City to room the thousands of factory workers during that period; and those who remained in the area eventually bought homes in other sections of Granite City, Madison and Venice. While between up to 15,000 Macedonians may have lived and worked in the area throughout the first two decades, it is more probable that the Macedonians population at any one time was between 2,000[177] and 6,000.[178] By 1920, there were only between 1,500 and 2,000 Macedonians remaining in Granite City, Madison, Venice and St. Louis.[179]

Most of these immigrants to southwestern Illinois and St. Louis were unskilled migrant workers that provided a steady stream of cheap labor for the mills and foundries. However, some men arrived with intentions of remaining there forever and becoming important fixtures in their communities. Christ Anastasoff, who authored *The Tragic Peninsula*, became significantly involved in his St. Louis community at a young age. In the summer of 1924, at the age of 27, he ran for a congressional seat under the Socialist Labor Party ticket.[180] In 1926, he ran under the same ticket for a state senate seat.[181]

Another Macedonian from St. Louis was Vladimir Kanazireff. Kanazireff was originally from Razlog, Pirin Macedonia, and by 1930s he had become a school teacher at a St. Louis high school. As he noted, he was brought up on the Macedonian revolution. He described his revolutionary work to the *St. Louis Post-Dispatch* in 1934:

**I have been in America for 12 years. I have outgrown my hatreds and my early chauvinism. Now I can admit that we, too, have made mistakes. I have seen such paradoxes. A priest with a cross in one hand and a Bible in the other, this standing for charity and that**

saying 'you must not kill', leading a regiment into battle, running before them to the slaughter.[182]

Kanazireff was bitter about Turkish oppression. He described how "Macedonians had to wear a distinctive sash and walk in the streets with their heads bowed and their hands in a supplicating attitude." Kanazireff's father was a politically prominent person and acted as an emissary to the Turkish provincial authorities. His father sent him to military college in Sofia where for the first time he "acquired a deep love for the Bulgarians and strengthened his antipathy for Greeks, Serbs and Turks." Kanazireff later explained this affinity toward Bulgaria: "The Macedonians were reconciled to identifying themselves with Bulgaria if they could break the oppressive yoke of Turkey."[183]

After the failed revolution, a brother-in-law in America offered to support him while he studied to become a diplomat. Therefore, Kanazireff came to Granite City. However, the depression of 1907 struck the city with a mighty blow and his brother-in-law went bankrupt. With no financial help in America, Kanazireff earned a living by tutoring students in French. He eventually left Granite City and traveled to Paris, where he engaged in diplomatic studies for a while. However, the Balkan Wars broke out and Kanazireff went back to fight in the wars. After the wars, he returned to Paris and graduated from university in 1914. He was appointed as Bulgaria's consul to St. Petersburg, Russia; but that position only lasted a few months because Bulgaria barged into the First World War as a German ally. During the war, Kanazireff was Chief of Staff for the Occupation Brigade in Serbia. There, he was devastatingly shocked by how Macedonians were treated by both the Serbians and Bulgarians. He left Bulgaria, returned to the Granite City area, and became a teacher for a St. Louis high school.[184]

Other Macedonian immigrants in the area also desired to entertain politics and diplomacy. Take the case of Stoyu Stoyeff, for example. Stoyeff was an editor of *Naroden Glas* in Granite City and was well known for writing articles that advocated for an anarcho-socialist form of society. He told an immigration court during his application for naturalization how he would run the country. He called for the abolition of all government branches, including the executive, legislative and judiciary. He said he was in favor of ownership of industries by workers and a division of profits among them. Stoyeff insisted he was opposed to violent means in order to implement that agenda but would support all legal avenues in accomplishing that goal. The immigration authorities did not embrace his radical ideologies and opposed his application for citizenship.[185]

For Stoyan Christowe, who lived in St. Louis for a couple of years before carving a path that would lead to a seat in the Vermont Senate, menial factory labor further fueled his desire to pursue Americanization of the mind and soul, not simply just of the body and bank account. He compared his labor in those early years in St. Louis to village work in Macedonia:

**It seemed to me I was paid not so much for doing any hard work…as for not living. In the old country work was a part of living. Work and life were inextricably bound up. There was a union between the doer and the things done. When you pruned the vines you knew why you had to do it, and you could see the sap running from the eye of the slashed vine like tears from a human eye. When you swung the**

scythe in the meadow you heard the grass sigh as it fell in swaths at your feet. The scythe itself hissed like a snake as it devoured the flowery grass. Whatever you did in the old country you understood.[186]

Christowe eventually enrolled at Valparaiso University in Indiana, found work as a journalist, and authored several books before settling down in Vermont.

Of course, academia and politics were not common career fields for those early Macedonian immigrants. Most toiled away in the foundries and mills. Still, the thousands of Macedonians working 12-hour shifts required that their basic needs be met, and plenty of other Macedonians utilized their skills from the old country to serve those needs. Bakeries, grocery stores, meat markets, restaurants and other types of businesses sprouted as soon as there was a large enough immigrant customer base. The following are just some of the businesses established by Macedonians:

- John Tarpoff and Krste Evangeloff from Garbesh operated a meat market in Granite City.[187]
- D. N. Popovsky in Madison had a calendar company called the Popovsky Calendar Company.[188]
- Dimitar Shecroff of Dumbeni opened a tailor shop in Madison.[189]
- C. P. Vershuroff started a money agency in Granite City with the slogan: "Money for the Old Country!"[190]
- Krste Kolev of Banica owned the Macedonian Commercial Company; it included a saloon, hotel, and restaurant.[191]

- Misho Mitseff of Surovichevo opened a market and restaurant in Granite City.[192]
- George Tsvetkovich from Slupche established a bakery in Granite City.[193]
- The Zhuglovi brothers from Vambel opened the Saloon Viaduct Buffet in St. Louis, which included a hotel, restaurant, poolroom and coffee house.[194]
- Josif Georgiev from Dihovo and Giche Olev from Banica operated Café Macedonia in Granite City.[195]
- James Lazaroff and Elio Spoyonoff operated the White Cheese Factory in Edwardsville.[196]
- Naum Marcovsky of Kosinec owned a meat market in Madison.[197]
- Naum Belkoff and Vasil Stavroff, both from Brznica, had a meat market and bakery in Madison.[198]
- Lazar Palcheff of Kosinec owned a large building in Madison that he built in 1906, and it served as a market and banking agency.[199]
- Sotir and Andrija Karandzhov from Smrdesh operated two candy shops in St Louis.[200]
- John Kliasheff, also from Smrdesh, operated the Balkan Café in Madison. An advertisement from 1922: "The most modern and oldest café...here you will meet the most intelligent people in our colony, and you can pass your time in peace."[201]
- Lambro Bitsoff from Kosinec was a tailor in Madison.
- Ivan D. Zaimov of Smrdesh owned the Sanitary Grocery & Meat Market in Madison.[202]
- V. N. Kalanovsky from Kosinec had a tailor shop in Granite City.[203]

- Georg Vasilev from Nestram owned the Blue Grass Buffet in St. Louis.[204]
- Luka Lovacheff and Jane Kirkoff of Drenoveni operated a market in Granite City.[205]
- Hristo Saimon and Vasil Jakov, Macedonians from Albania, operated the International Restaurant in Granite City.
- Kosta Nicoloff of Laktine operated the oldest market in St. Louis.[206]
- Paskal Siromahov and Mihail and Argir Londov, from Galishta, owned a candy shop in St. Louis.[207]
- Peter Georgieff had a 57-acre farm in Edwardsville where he made white cheese (Macedonian cheese).
- Dimitar Nicoloff (with roots from Serres, Demir Hisar, and Bitola) owned a bakery in Wood River.

In addition to the above, there were many saloons and coffeehouses operated by wealthier Macedonians, such as Alabach and Mitsareff. In St. Louis there were two Macedonian-owned coffeehouses in particular that Macedonians frequented in those early decades. One of them was Paskal's coffeehouse, called the Balkan. It was especially known as a gathering place for prominent socialists and communists in the area; these Macedonian leftists would gather every Sunday and denounce capitalism and offer their thoughts on how to reconstruct government and society. Other coffeehouses had belly dancers; but the Balkan was for the intelligentsia. Other coffeehouses had pool tables at the center of the floor; the Balkan's sole pool table was in a corner. Paskal discouraged people from wearing short sleeves or overalls in his establishment, unlike the other establishments, which had no dress code. He geared his coffeehouse to the enlightened and the intellectually curious; and on Sundays, those types of Macedonians from Madison, Granite City and Alton would come to the Balkan to talk politics and diplomacy. Paskal, who was born in Macedonia and raised in Sofia as a refugee, was one of the few Macedonians in St. Louis during that time who could read and understand the American newspapers.[208]

The typical Macedonian immigrant attitude toward reading the American newspapers, however, looked to the English language with indifference. The Macedonians anticipated that they would only be in America for a few years; learning English was not necessary and was usually considered a waste of time. Christowe's uncle relayed this message to his nephew one evening in St. Louis:

**And what good is English to you? Who'll pay you money for English? We didn't come here to learn English. We're here to work and save and go back home to live like human beings, as God meant we should live...How can we live decent lives here? ... Here we are something like they gypsies in our own country, who come and go. The Americans think of us as we think of the gypsies. The sooner we go back, the better.[209] ...**

**Yes, there's decent people in America. There's people here who live good lives. Who have homes and wives and children...The Americans will never give us the easy jobs. It'll be coal shoveling, engine wiping for us. You don't want to do that forever, do you? You can't strike roots here. You'll always be a stranger here. The *bumbi* think they're Americans because they learn a little English like parrots. How can they be Americans? Until yesterday they herded sheep and poked oxen and wore pigskin sandals. Because now they wear silk shirts and neckties and brown shoes and pantaloons and have gold on their**

**teeth, does that make them Americans? Clothes don't make Americans. ...**

**Until they came here they were lucky to eat cornbread and to sleep on straw mats on the ground. Now that they tasted white bread they want to eat in the restaurants. And to live on** *foornish* **and go to the theatricals, the electricals, and the lives ones. Now I can understand how it might be amusing to go to an electrical once and see photographs that move, but to go to a live show like the Standard where I hear women who have no shame come out without clothes on! That's bad!**[210]

Most Macedonians, indeed, only desired to make money in America so they could return to their families and villages. Many hardly wasted a dime on anything but the necessities and looked down on those who blew their money on lavish articles or frivolous and sinful entertainment. To them, being in America meant a few years of hard work in exchange for a lifetime of comfort and prosperity. The sacrifices that these Macedonian men made to accomplish this goal, however, were not trivial.

First, finding and maintaining employment in America was not always guaranteed. Yes, the wealthy labor agents often found work for Macedonians. When the American economy was strong, this was easy. However, when national and regional depressions took grip, the immigrants were the first to feel the ill effects. Moreover, shady labor agents and foremen in factories would often sell positions to the immigrants. An Irishman named Frank in St. Louis, for example, worked as a foreman at the roundhouses there. He openly accepted bribes in exchange for the most coveted positions.[211] Across the Mississippi at the American Steel Foundry in Granite City,

Licho Evanoff was charged with operating an employment bureau without a license in 1914. Along with four American foremen, he was prosecuted for selling jobs to applicants. Many immigrants testified at court they had to pay him to get a job.[212] Thus, often a Macedonian had to relinquish part of his salary just to keep his job.

One such story of being duped by a labor agent was reported in detail in the press. In May of 1908, Tanas Dimeff paid a Macedonian labor agent $5 for a job in Arkansas. Dimeff then bought a railroad ticket with the rest of his money. He worked at the railroad camp in Arkansas for a month, but his employer told him that he would not pay Dimeff even though he owed him $16. Dimeff knew he had been cheated; so, without any money, he began his trip back to Granite City, the only place where he knew he could find other Macedonians.[213]

He started his trip with three loaves of rye bread, carrying the bread on a stick over his shoulder. Those lasted him five days. He then slogged along for two days without food. After he could no longer walk due to weakness, he approached a house, pointed to his mouth, and spoke the only English word he knew: bread. The owner shooed him away. He visited several more homes before he was finally offered a meal.[214]

Dimeff then continued on his way, but soon collapsed from exhaustion on a village street. The people there fed him and gave him enough food to last him to Kansas City. He found a Macedonian baker there and stayed with him for two days. The baker gave Dimeff four loaves, and the young Macedonian started out again for Granite City. When he reached St. Louis, he was so exhausted that a policeman found him slouched over on a street, fed him, and gave him five cents to pay the toll to cross the bridge.[215]

At noon, Dimeff arrived in Granite City, tumbling onto the porch of Nick Alabach's saloon. The patrons inside saw him, and one man exclaimed: "It's Dimeff!" They crowded around him and asked dozens of questions. He just pointed to his mouth and said "bread." Dimeff then relayed his story through Shoomkoff. "I wouldn't care, only my feet went to pieces," said Dimeff. Shoomkoff then highlighted how the labor agents take advantage of the Macedonians:

**It is a shame the way our people are treated. The labor agents rob them. They promise them good jobs in some faraway place, and when they get there they are worked for a month and then are not paid. As they cannot speak English and are ignorant of the ways of this country, they submit to the injustice. Not long ago 27 of them who had been so treated walked all the way back from Arkansas. The Federal Government ought to take it up, for it is a great injustice.[216]**

The federal government eventually did get involved through Seraphis' investigation. Other times, Macedonians took it upon themselves to confront their abusers. When the Macedonians felt they were being duped by their American employers, they organized strikes. In March of 1909, 200 Macedonians, Bulgarians and Greeks went on strike at the American Steel Works in Granite City. They demanded a raise of 25 cents per day. However, their demands went ignored because they were easily replaceable.[217]

Even non-Macedonian bankers tried to take advantage of the Macedonians. In 1917, the Illinois Supreme Court ruled in favor of Ilio Simonoff in a case against the Granite City National

Bank. Ilio had purchased drafts from the bank in May of 1914 totaling almost $1,500. His brother Sotir was returning to his home in Macedonia and expected to receive the money once he reached France. However, Sotir was drafted into the Serbian army before he could visit Paris. Therefore, Sotir's friend, Theodore Illoff, carried the drafts back with him to Granite City and handed them to Simonoff.[218]

At Granite City National Bank, Simonoff presented the drafts for a refund. The war had caused a decrease in the exchange rate and the bank only returned to Simonoff $1,380 instead of the entire $1,500. The Illinois Supreme Court ruled that Granite City National Bank had to pay the full value of the drafts, even though the Madison County Court judge and the Appellate Court in Mount Vernon ruled in favor of the bank.[219]

This recession, however, effected the Macedonians in more than one way. Because Macedonians possessed fewer skills and connections than their American neighbors, and because they had a poor grasp of the English language, employment was scarce during economic downturns. Cities, nonprofits and state governments therefore rallied behind the Macedonians and other immigrants to keep them afloat. For example, in late April of 1908, the mayors of Granite City, Madison and Venice agreed to duplicate a $250 contribution by the township supervisor for the "1,500 Bulgarians, Roumanians and Macedonians" jobless in Granite City.[220]

In May of that year, many American clergymen and missionaries met at the Niedringhaus Memorial Methodist Church in Madison to create a committee to oversee the needs of over 1,700 foreigners, "mostly Bulgarians and Macedonians," who had lost their jobs in the Tri-Cities. Those on the committee included Reverend C. C. Hall of Niedringhaus Church; Reverend Milton Page of the First Presbyterian Church; T. S. Bagranoff, a Presbyterian missionary; and missionaries P. S. Basileff and W. J. Lynch. Illinois Governor Charles Deneen also advocate for the jobless immigrants. He found work for 50 of them with the Chicago Street Railway Company, and then encouraged Burlington Railway to promise work for 100 more. The one stipulation was that whoever received employment through the governor's efforts had to donate $1 every week to assist the jobless Macedonians. At the meeting in Niedringhaus, the Ladies Aid Societies of various churches were acquiring and providing provisions for 500 of the foreigners, while bakers and grocers in the Tri-Cities had joined efforts to care for the needs of the 1,200 others. Governor Deneen also asked the legislature to appropriate money to care for the foreigners. He had been allowed $5,000 per year for that specific purpose, but because of the economic decline, that money had been exhausted by spring.[221]

This support for Macedonians and other foreigners bothered many Americans. One who resented this free support for non-natives wrote a letter to the newspaper expressing his frustration:

**I don't think there are one out of ten of the Americans that are doing anything. My neighbors are all idle, and myself as well. And we have walked the shoes off our feet looking for work, but failed. But I see from your paper that the Bulgarians and Macedonians have got Gov. Deneen looking for work for them. And they also have the sympathy of the Christians of Granite City. How is it that they give no thought to the American man? Your paper says the Americans are well-cared for and have work, but I know this is not true. Everything here is**

shut down but the stamping and glucose works, and they hire Greeks and Bulgarians mostly, so how could the Americans have work. The American citizen has always been proud of his citizenship, but it won't be long at this rate till he will be ashamed of his identity. What these Americans want is work, not confidence.[222]

This general resentment toward the Macedonians and other immigrants often caused problems between Americans and Macedonians, which occasionally resulted in physical altercations. For example, several hundred Macedonians and Americans fought with one another on several occasions beginning in 1906. A major brawl between them transpired on September 15 at the American Steel Foundry – over 700 men were involved.[223]

The brawl started on Saturday night after an American blamed his malaria infection on immigrant Macedonians. A Macedonian heard the remark and charged him with an iron bar. He was about to strike him when other Americans rushed to their compatriot's defense. Macedonians and other immigrant workers then rushed to defend the Macedonian. The scene was a wild one. A night supervisor saw a Macedonian sprint by him during the fight screaming that there was a riot going on in the north end of the building as an American wielding a hammer chased him down. The Macedonians were outnumbered two to one, which proved fatal in a fight with guns, hammers, iron rods and all sorts of metal tools. One Macedonian was killed; Christo Tolo was shot in the back; Vassil Pedro had his eye "jabbed out"; Stano Pedro had a fractured rib and scalp wounds; and Kukanokus broke his wrist. Several more would have likely perished had the police not rushed in with their revolvers drawn, which scattered the crowd.[224]

The Macedonians retreated because they were outnumbered. They withdrew to Hungary Hollow, gathered hundreds of Macedonians, and returned to the foundry with those reinforcements. They attempted to get into the foundry, but the gates were barred. The superintendent of the company promised the Macedonians protection for them when they came back to work on Monday. Indeed, on that Monday, the Granite City police swore in 200 deputies to prevent another brawl at the factory.[225]

A second way in which Macedonians sacrificed much, in order to save money, revolved around their living arrangements. By 1905, of the thousands of Macedonians living in Granite City and its surroundings, only four were there with their families. The Macedonians often lived in a bachelor boarding system: up to 20 or more immigrants in a rented house or apartment. Many of these rooming houses were operated by owners of saloons or grocery stores and cost between five and eight dollars per months.[226] Most of these boarding houses had two or three floors or were cottages with three or four rooms. The first floor was almost always some sort of mercantile establishment. There were ten large boarding establishments in the area that housed up to 500 residents.[227]

The men in St. Louis, on the other hand, lived 12 to a flat. There were six cots in a flat, occupied by six men during the day and six different men at night while the day-roomers worked in the mills. The cots were without bedsheets and the blankets were grimy from coal dust, oil and grease. The flat's kitchen had no running water, sink or drain; water was brought up with buckets from a tap in the yard and dishes were washed on the porch. The total rent was six dollars per month; or, 50 cents per occupant. Board, which included two meals a day, cost four dollars per month. The only other food that Macedonians regularly bought was round loaves of bread from nearby Macedonian bakers, which cost a nickel per loaf.[228] In this manner, the frugal Macedonians sacrificed decent living conditions so they could save as much money as possible.

Americans in the area and government officials were repulsed by how Macedonians and other immigrants lived in these tight quarters. Many sanitary laws and ordinances were thus enacted to crack down on unsanitary communal living. In East St. Louis in 1907, nearly 50 Macedonians, Hungarians, Austrians and Greeks were arrested for violating the city's sanitary ordinances because they were living in crowded and unclean quarters. A Macedonian community representative paid each of their fines and the men were released.[229]

The living conditions in St. Louis – a much larger city – and the targeting of immigrants there were much worse than in Granite City. In St. Louis, many bakeries were owned by Macedonians. By February of 1908, the city's health inspectors began cracking down on them. A description of Phillip Christ's bakery on South Street stated: "Two bakers made 500 loaves of bread every night, which were sold among the Macedonians in the quarter over the counter of the store and peddled in baskets to whoever would buy." The bread was made in a room behind a poorly furnished storefront, and the room in the back was only 250 square feet. There was an oven in the wall at one end of the room and two outhouses in the yard behind it.

During the time of inspection, six men were lounging about the room, smoking cigarettes. The Macedonian working at the bread was dressed in dirty clothes and was also smoking. A cot was nestled in the other corner of the room where he slept. The shovels used were encrusted with black dirt and looked like they had never been cleaned.[230]

Pete Lazaro's bakery was worse. One half of the bakery was described as being used for mixing dough and baking it into bread, while the other half served as a boarding house, with three beds, a stove, table, chairs and walls covered with clothes. A cat was asleep in a bread tray close to some of the bread loaves. There was no ventilation. Windows were so dirty that light could not "penetrate the grime on the glass." Further, the inspector noted:

**They said they were Macedonians, and that two bakers turned out about 400 loaves of bread every night, which were peddled in the neighborhood from baskets. ... The examples given here are all in one district and do not comprise all the bakeries in it conducted by Macedonians, who seem to be the only bread bakers in that part of the city. Some bakeries in the Ghetto district are even worse than these. ... Some of them are indescribably dirty and utterly unsanitary, and their product is harmful to the general health of the consumers, as well as being a carrier of the germs of consumption and other diseases.[231]**

A newspaper article even referred to this living condition as evil: "One of the greatest evils of the unclean bakeshops is the practice of using a portion of the baking room as a lodging house. The Greeks and Macedonians are more given to this practice than are the Jews and Italians of the Ghetto."[232]

In March 1908, Health Inspector Sikes introduced a bill for the regulation of these bakeries and several public hearings were held. The Legislative Committee of the City Council was not satisfied with the bill or the investigation into the bakeries, and they strongly objected to a clause that would force bakers to undergo a health examination by the Board of Health. They considered this "class legislation". Sikes responded that this was the most important clause of the bill:

**Why should not bakers who make one of the principal articles of food be made to keep in good health and clean as barbers? There are many consumptives among bakers, and I have had an uphill fight against them ever since I have been in this work. Can anyone imagine a greater menace to the public health than to have a baker with consumption working in the dough that goes into bread eaten by the public? ...**

**The bakers put up the false argument that if they should be examined as to the condition of their health then grocers, butchers and everyone who handled foodstuffs should be examined. The answer to that is clear. Any person patronizing grocers and butchers can go into their shops and see for themselves whether the person who serves him has consumption and refuse to patronize him. This is not the case with men who work in dough in underground and filthy bakeries. But the abattoirs and small slaughter houses are rigidly inspected both by the Government and the State. There are many trades which have to undergo inspection. ...**

**It would be extremely unjust to say that all small bakeries are unclean, because most of them, particularly those conducted by Germans, are models of cleanliness. It is the bakeries in the districts inhabited by the Italians, Jews, Greeks and Macedonians which are the ones that need stringent regulation. If a man is in good health he should not object to going before the Board of Health four times a**

**year and getting a certificate. If he is not in good health he has no business working in a bakery anyway.**[233]

Many Americans today cannot fathom living and working in such conditions. Cleanliness is a daily ritual for most and many would not even be able to tolerate rooms without running water or toilets. Health and sanitary standards have certainly improved. For the early Macedonian immigrants, however, minimalist living was the rule of thumb if they wanted to return to Macedonia with pockets full of cash.

However, sometimes even minimalist living could not guarantee that they would be returning to Macedonia with their hard-earned money. Many Americans and immigrants alike knew that Macedonians carried their money on them – whether in their shoes, their pockets, their wallets, or in some secret clothing compartment. Thieves thus pounced on these Macedonians like cats pouncing on mice in a bakery: every single day.

# FIVE
# Money is Dangerous

Although most Macedonians did not splurge while in America, this new land was attractive and idyllic in many ways. Many missed their families, villages and outdoor lifestyle in Macedonia, but America was overflowing with amenities, technologies, comforts, and opportunities unheard of in Macedonia. Moreover, there were freedoms and rights in America, concepts foreign to the Christian Macedonians in Muslim-occupied Macedonia. And while America was not free of crime, it at least had a respectable mechanism for delivering justice. For Macedonians in Granite City who hoarded their cash, this justice system was welcomed, as they were frequently targeted by thieves and robbers.

Targeted on more than one occasion was Gosheff, who, like many other wealthy individuals, was always in the sights of schemers. On September 27, 1909, for example, Gosheff drove his horse and wagon to St. Louis and loaded the wagon with goods, such as safety pins and bedsteads, valued at $175. A thief stole his wagon, horse and goods while he was rummaging about in a store making further purchases. Someone later found the horse and wagon, but none of the goods.[234]

Another Macedonian merchant, Nicola, was shot and killed in his store in 1906 after being robbed of $160. Johan Platko was the only witness. He was drawn to the two robbers because they were African-American, and African-Americans were rarely spotted in Hungary Hollow. Platko crept to the window of the store and saw them walk toward Nicola with a threatening gesture. He heard: "Give up your money, quick!" They pulled out a revolver, Nicola fell, and the robbers left, firing at the boy on their way out and speeding toward the African-American colony east of Granite City.[235]

The boy ran to Peter Radcliffe's store down the street, who rushed to the scene with his bartender, both men wielding their revolvers. Two nearby policemen saw the robbers trying to escape and they continued running even after they were ordered to halt. The police chased after them but were fired upon by the men. They lost the robbers, but the $160 in money included 45 *napoleons*, a 5-*franc* piece, and a *ruble*. The police issued a notice for residents to be on the lookout for any African-Americans trying to exchange such money.[236]

One of Mitsareff's businesses was also targeted. In 1908, two brothers, John and Joseph Csehi, were arrested for attempting to rob Mitsareff's saloon in Hungary Hollow. At 11:00 p.m. on a Monday, the brothers refused to pay for their drinks. Mitsareff insisted they pay, but the men then tried to hold up Mitsareff, who grabbed a gun and opened fire at them. Those shots attracted a police officer. Ten shots in total were fired between all three parties. The brothers were captured after being shot in the legs.[237]

In a 1909 robbery of two Macedonian brothers, Space and Petre Anastasoff, the newspapers were astonished by how much money the men had earned and saved in just a few years. The two brothers together earned $90 per month and had amassed $1,300 in just over two years. That money was stolen from them in a robbery. At first, the police officers were bewildered at how the brothers could have saved such a large sum in such a short time. An interpreter talked about their frugality and that they had even sent several hundreds of dollars to relatives in Macedonia prior to being robbed. One policeman said: "No wonder there's no money in circulation."[238]

As the years progressed, the thieves became creative. For example, in December of 1929, three armed men posing as prohibition agents entered Christ Koless' pickled pepper establishment in Granite City. They served him a warrant and demanded he hand over $1,900. For good measure, they kidnapped his 12-year-old son Vasil and escaped by automobile, throwing the boy out of the car in Madison. Koless had formerly owned a saloon, but once prohibition came into effect, he entered the pickled pepper business and built up a nationwide trade, mostly dealing "with Macedonians and Bulgarians." He normally had a lot of money in his establishment on Saturdays to cash customers' paychecks. The robbers knew this.[239]

A similar scenario transpired two years later. Macedonians George Evangeloff, a saloonkeeper in Madison, and N. V. Marcovsky, a grocer, were robbed of $1,900 by three men posing as prohibition agents. The Macedonians were returning from Granite City with money to cash payroll checks for customers when Evangeloff's car was "crowded to the curb" by another car. Two men came out, displayed badges, and announced they were prohibition agents. They then drew revolvers and ordered the two in the rear seats. They drove to Eagle Park, south of Madison, and took Evangeloff's money and car keys.[240]

In another instance, Christ Pashoff, manager of Washington Theater in Granite City, and James Kostoff, doorman at the City Theater in Granite City, were robbed of $285 "by a couple of pretty good fellows." Pashoff had just locked his theater and was getting into his car when robbers demanded money from him. He had nothing and they forced him to take them back into the theater. Pashoff explained that the police had the key to the safe containing the theater's receipts. At that instant, Kostoff happened to visit Pashoff and asked if he wanted to get a cup of coffee. Losing their patience, the robbers forced Kostoff into the theater and Pashoff pried open a safe with $275 in silver. Another safe contained an envelope with $50. Pashoff told the robbers that the $50 was for the Red Cross, and the men put the envelope back into the safe. "We don't want Red Cross money," one said. They searched Pashoff and took a few more dollars from him. They turned to Kostoff, who said he did not make much money. So, they said: "Okay, we'll split it with you." They took two $5 bills and left him six $1 bills, but missed $80 that was hidden in a secret compartment in his wallet. The robbers then said: "We'll tie you up with this twine, but you won't have a hard time breaking it. It will keep you here just long enough for us to get away."[241]

Of course, not all robbers were that kind. In November of 1908, a stranger poisoned and robbed five Macedonians in St. Louis. At a saloon attached to a house, a man with gold teeth, a scar on his cheek, and an unusually long nose, freely bought beer for the Macedonians. He then asked if he could sleep in the house because he feared he would be robbed of the hundreds of dollars in his possession. The men were quickly put to sleep, not realizing they had been drugged, and the crook got away with $227. When the Macedonians awoke, the man and their money were gone. One of the Macedonians, Forta Sotar, died while being rushed to the hospital.[242]

Several years later, A. V. Andreoff, secretary-treasurer of a Madison bank, was robbed while working as the sole cashier that day. Two men had entered in an aimless fashion and Andreoff suspected they were up to no good, so he went behind the caged teller's space. They asked him for bank checks, but then a third man entered, drew a revolver and ordered him to put his hands up. Another man jumped into the cage and struck Andreoff on the shoulder with the revolver. Andreoff said: "Take all the money you want, it's insured, but don't hit me." But they continued to beat him, hitting him on the head and back. The robbers scooped all the money from three drawers into a sack and then ordered Andreoff to open the wall safe, but it was empty. A customer came in and was ordered to lie on the floor.[243]

Two men outside named George Barokevich and Elia Christoff saw the men enter. When the would-be robbers exited the car, they confronted Barokevich and yelled at him to come over to them. He feared for his life and instead ran into a dry goods store; he found a hiding spot and told the owner, Steve Dimitroff, that men were robbing the bank. One of the robbers followed Barokevich into the store, bought a 10-cent handkerchief, and upon entering the bank muttered to Christoff, who was still outside: "Sit still, you, or we'll shoot your head off." They ran out of the bank shooting in every direction, but no one was shot.[244]

Macedonians constantly feared being robbed and notoriously assumed that everyone was out to get them: they trusted nobody. On one occasion, the McKinley Traction

Company could not furnish the Tri-Cities with light during the evening because its employees had gone on strike. Private detectives were then sent to patrol the railroad tracks near the company. Four Macedonians in Madison were on their way to work that night, walking alongside the tracks, when one of these detectives halted them. The Macedonians did not understand English and assumed the man was trying to rob them, so they beat him up. He was sent to the hospital and charged with carrying concealed weapons; meanwhile, the Macedonians were given a pass.[245]

Macedonians were not only targets of robberies. In the 1930s, a streak of bombings in St. Louis did not spare Macedonians. Lambro Shmagranoff's wholesale pastry bake shop, for example, was attacked by dynamite. He was sleeping on a cot in the office in order to be near his business when dynamite exploded and damaged his truck and threw him off his cot. The explosion was heard over a mile away, shattering 25 windows in five buildings. Shmagranoff said that a year ago he was visited by men who asked him to unionize his shop, and he said he would do so only when other shops became unionized. He said he received no threats. This was the 12th such bombing in St. Louis in 1934.[246]

Occasionally, Macedonians did find themselves on the other side of the law. On April 29, 1909, Traico Lazoff, a young Macedonian, was arrested in Granite City by U.S. Deputy Marshal Addleman for perjury when applying for admission into the U.S. He was thus returned to New York for deportation. He had been a fugitive from the western district of New York, escaped into Canada, and came back to Buffalo after a year. He was identified shortly after getting employment with the American Steel Foundry in Granite City.[247]

Other times, the crimes were a little more severe. Simon Helojian and John Petroneff, two Macedonians from Granite City, were arguing so loudly about a personal matter that traffic was impeded in Hungary Hollow on a spring day in 1911. The two were about to engage in a duel when police arrived and arrested Simon.[248]

A decade later, a Macedonian participated in a duel with an American and both men were killed. At a soft drink parlor in Madison, Tony Vellkoff and the American man named Frank quarreled over an unknown matter. Around 20 people – mostly Macedonians – were inside the establishment at the time.[249] The two decided to have a duel: Vellkoff fired first, then Frank fired; then the men started firing wildly and the patrons ran for cover. Two Macedonians were injured in the exchange. A man named George then drove away with Frank's body and dumped it in a 12-foot embankment between Venice and Brooklyn. George then fled the area.[250]

Finally, although rare, some Macedonians were doing the robbing and the murdering themselves. In September of 1911, Antonas Lazoff confessed to Minnesota police for the murder of Christo Georgeoff at the Commonwealth Steel Foundry in Granite City several months prior. Lazoff disappeared from Granite City after Georgeoff was found shot and robbed on a railway track. A Macedonian in Granite City said that Lazoff had told him about how he was planning on going to Minnesota just before Georgeoff was killed.[251]

Macedonians often found themselves victims rather than perpetrators of crimes. Usually, their saving habits made them perfect targets for thieves and robbers. Eventually, Macedonians in Granite City would entrust their money to the wealthy Macedonian bankers in town. However, these bankers were not always reliable, as seen in Mitsareff's case.

But although securing their money until their return trip to Macedonia was often a challenging task, Macedonians found safety in numbers. They may not have been in Macedonia, but they certainly brought Macedonia with them to Granite City.

# SIX
# The Macedonian Spirit

By 1903, several Macedonians had trickled into Granite City and St. Louis. While there was not yet any organized society advocating for their interests, they were immediately infused into a region that was teeming with immigrants, of whom many were sympathetic to the Macedonian Cause. One of these pro-Macedonian advocates was Reverend John Nekula, a pastor at the Saint Wenceslaus Bohemian Catholic Church in St. Louis. Reverend Nekula was born in Moravia (Czech Republic) in 1871. He immigrated to America, became pastor of St. Wenceslaus in 1901, and was regarded as a man of influence, both in the St. Louis area and in the Czech community.[252]

In the late summer of 1903, Reverend Nekula visited Bulgaria and Macedonia to observe the conditions in Macedonia. IMRO had initiated their long-awaited insurrection against the Turkish army in early August; and while the Macedonians were victorious in many initial battles, numerous reports poured in describing the excesses and cruelties committed by the Sultan's forces. Upon returning to St. Louis in September, Nekula began speaking to the public on the Macedonian situation. In one speech, he focused particularly on the common Christian cause of the Macedonians, Serbians and Bulgarians. He said:

**Already many of the best officers of the army of these countries [Bulgaria and Serbia] have resigned to accept commissions with the Macedonians, and the announcement that war was declared against**

the Turks, would be hailed with the delight by the armed forces of both of the countries named. The Bulgarians and Servians have many interests in common with the persecuted people, principally their religion. Both nations were once under Turkish rule, and they understand fully what their friends are now enduring.[253]

Nekula was certainly not the only pastor in the Granite City area to deliver sermons on the plights of the Macedonians and how the Macedonian Christians needed the support of Europe's and America's Christian brethren. Yet, he was an early voice for the Macedonian people in the region that translated the Macedonian point-of-view to a relatively uninformed American public. To Nekula, the Macedonians were separate but equal to their neighbors and friends, the Serbians and Bulgarians.

Within a couple of years, the Macedonian population in Granite City exploded and Macedonians began forming their own societies, instituting their own newspapers, and utilizing their own pastors, doctors and intellectuals to advocate on behalf of their own interests. These Macedonians then assumed the role of communicating the plight and needs of Macedonians to an unknowledgeable American public.

For example, Shoomkoff, who earned his doctoral degree from the University of Pennsylvania after graduating from the University of Chicago, was one of these early Macedonian advocates. Not only was he editor of Alabach's *Macedonia* and served as counsel to Macedonians facing legal trouble, he delivered many speeches on the Macedonian Question. Speaking in 1903, he was brutally honest with his Macedonian faction's aims:

**It may seem strange to say we are not trying to form a government in Macedonia. But such is the fact; our warfare is conducted simply with a view to force Bulgaria to fight Turkey. Her people are doing it, with food, recruits, arms and funds, but her government has stood like the rest of the powers and looked on.**[254]

Shoomkoff was a Sarafov supporter and thus it is no surprise he was itching for Bulgaria to attack Turkey. Sarafov had convinced many that if the Macedonians revolted against the Turks, the Bulgarian army would immediately swoop in and assist them. Delchev, Sandanski and other autonomists had opposed and discredited such delusions.

Christo Nedelkoff, the eventual editor of the rival Macedonian newspaper in Granite City, *Naroden Glas*, resided in Chicago before he found his way to Granite City. Around the same time as Shoomkoff was appealing for aid from the American public, Nedelkoff was explaining why Macedonians in Illinois were staging war drills. "All we fear is that the Turkish government will compel the United States to disarm us," he said. "That would delay us considerably, although every Macedonian would make his way out of the country and reach the scene of action." He explained that the Macedonians must be prepared for war.[255]

A few years later, in October of 1907, *Naroden Glas* sprouted to life, several months after *Macedonia* had taken root in Granite City. Unlike *Macedonia*, which took a more autonomist and nationalist approach to the Macedonian Question, *Naroden Glas* was a socialist publication for the Macedonians and Bulgarians. Nedelkoff announced its purpose to an America public and to explain why some Macedonians had difficulty adjusting to American life:

> Most of the Macedonians in Granite City and Madison are political refugees from Turkey....the two peoples [Bulgarians and Macedonians], as a whole, are orderly and law-abiding. Whatever infractions of laws have taken place among them are due to their ignorance of the law, or their misunderstanding as to what constitutes freedom.

Nedelkoff then assured people the newspaper would help instruct readers what was meant by freedom.[256]

By 1908, Granite City was crowded with Macedonians, and respectable Macedonian and Balkan officials were often frequenting the city to address the crowds. P. N. Daskaloff of the *Vetcherna Poshta* in Sofia delivered one such address to a crowd of several hundred Macedonians and Bulgarians. He talked much about the situation in Macedonia and was received with generous applause. He described the conditions of Macedonia and emphasized the cruelty of the Sultan's troops; he exclaimed that many soldiers would be needed if Macedonia was to overthrow the Turkish empire and appealed to Macedonians and Bulgarians to prepare for such an occasion. In attendance at this speech were the rival newspaper editors, Nedelkoff and Shoomkoff.[257]

Just a few months later, 10,000 Macedonians from around the country met in a natural amphitheater in Granite City alongside the Mississippi River to draft some resolutions on the situation in Macedonia. As a result of this meeting, they sent cablegrams and telegrams to President Theodore Roosevelt, Sir Edward Grey (British Foreign Minister), and the Macedonian Committee in Sofia. The message to President Roosevelt asked him to support Macedonian autonomy and thanked him for hospitality extended to the Macedonians in America. To Sir Edward Grey, they begged him to convince the European powers to urge the Sultan to give Macedonia a Christian governor. And the message to Sofia said that Macedonians in America were ready to do everything possible to obtain freedom for Macedonia. Many of the Macedonians at the meeting were political refugees of Turkey and former IMRO rebels and were thus itching for Macedonia's freedom and the Sultan's overthrow.[258]

Their time finally came on the eve of the First Balkan War. On October 29, 1912, over 500 Macedonians and Bulgarians left Granite City to participate in the war against Turkey to liberate Macedonia. About 150 of them left in the morning, another 150 at noon, and 200 in the evening. For each trainload of Macedonians that departed, large crowds cheered them on. The morning started with a parade led by the Macedono-Bulgaro band, and they marched with Balkan and American flags through Hungary Hollow until the first train arrived. Many of the men were in military uniform and were carrying their guns with them. The event was described as 12 hours of singing war songs and general merrymaking festivities. The Macedonians even sang patriotic American songs, such as "America" and "Rally Round the Flag." A reporter wrote about the occasion: "Men who had come from the 'old country' together five years ago, had worked side by side and had been roommates ever since, were called upon to say good-bye to each other for the first time and perhaps the last." It was announced that 500 more men were expected to depart from Granite City for Macedonia by the end of the week. The American foundries and mills, however, were not pleased: they had to cope with the loss of the Macedonians by hiring Americans at twice the rate of pay than the Macedonians were given.²⁵⁹

Turkey lost that First Balkan War in February of 1913 and the Balkan communities of Granite City and St. Louis celebrated extensively. About 50 men who had lived in Granite City and Madison were killed in the war, and another 150 were wounded. Vasil Grammaticoff, an editor of *Naroden Glas* at the time, described the moment a Macedonian in Granite City received a letter from his brother who had been serving in the war:

**The brother assembled his friends, who crowded the tiny room in a tenement almost to suffocation. The only light was furnished by a toy coal of lamp, which filled the room with ill-smelled fumes. The scholar of the gathering, a boy who had learned to read in a mission school, took his place with dignity at a bare table. The other stood about. Their eyes shone in the gloom. With a blackened forefinger the youth laboriously read out the letters and read the words aloud. As he proceeded grimy fists smote the table, guttural exclamations of joy were uttered and burst of rough triumphant laughter resounded. When he finished all spoke excitedly and mustaches were fiercely twirled[.]²⁶⁰**

In the age of handwritten communication and in a community where only a few individuals were literate, this is how most correspondences with the homeland transpired during the time.

To be clear, the Macedonians were not always united. There were different camps at different times: those who were pro-Bulgarian against those who were pro-Macedonian; those who were nationalists against those who were socialists; those who were Sarafov supporters against those who were Sandanski supporters; and those who backed Shoomkoff and *Macedonia* against those who supported *Naroden Glas*. These divisions were highlighted at a trial during 1909 in which Reverend P. D. Vasileff, a minister at the Methodist Episcopal Church, filed suit against Victor S. Setchenoff and Vasil Stephanoff, editor of *Naroden Glas*, for libel because of an article they published that discredited Vasileff's character and work as a protestant minister. The St. Louis Post-Dispatch even reported that "the colony [was] split into factions and champions of both sides attended the trial."[261]

Unusual at this trial was that, when the witnesses took the stand, they inexplicably remained quiet and unable to speak. For example, Kluss Goncheff, who had told police and prosecutors his story about what had transpired several days before, was unable to formulate sentences when he took the stand. Shoomkoff had positioned himself in the court room so that he was in direct sight of Goncheff. This happened with other witnesses. A Macedonian then shouted that Shoomkoff was hypnotizing the witnesses and that was why they could not or would not speak. The prosecutor then demanded that Shoomkoff be arrested. The judge refused, saying that no legal grounds existed for such a charge. The prosecutor was then forced to drop the case because he found it impossible to now present evidence. The opposing factions were at a near brawl once the incident occurred in court,[262] and it was more probable that intimidation, rather the hypnosis, kept the witnesses quiet.

Still, the disputes between Macedonians were relatively minor and the bigger problems existed between Macedonians,

Greeks and Bulgarians. Most of the violence between the communities had evaporated by the 1910s, but the Balkan Wars and World War I certainly reignited negative feelings between them. For example, in the autumn of 1915, a major rift had divided the Macedonians and the Bulgarians. In late November, Alabach put on a fundraiser to raise money for the Red Cross in Macedonia and Bulgaria. A mass meeting of Macedonians and Bulgarians had netted $1,500. The Macedono-Bulgaro band was present, but the band members, too, were divided in their Macedonian and Bulgarian camps. Some of the festivity's attendees appealed to Alabach to help the two sides come to a truce so that there would be music at the event. Alabach sat down with the two sides and managed to draw out a truce between the Macedonians and Bulgarians, who agreed to put their differences aside for the time being and play for the festivities.[263]

Later in that decade, as the First World War concluded and the number of Macedonians in Granite City dwindled to a modest 1,500, the Macedonians there held another mass meeting. They adopted a resolution that on the Paris Peace Conference to aid in instituting a plebiscite in Macedonia. They also sent a letter to Illinois senators urging them to advocate for Macedonia's right to self-determination.[264]

Macedonians in Granite City and its surroundings were certainly politically active. Some, however, insisted that these immigrants were not realty Macedonians, ethnically, but rather Bulgarians and Greeks. The available evidence, including newspaper articles, census data and immigration records, tends to prove that most did identify as Macedonians and viewed themselves as different from others. Furthermore, and perhaps just as importantly, their American neighbors viewed them as Macedonians and their language as Macedonian, as evidenced in these advertisements that sought people who knew how to speak Macedonian. "Who can read and write English," one said, "and can speak Macedonian, Bulgarian, Polish and Turkish or Armenian."[265] Another said that he was "25 years of age, speaks, reads and writes English, German, French, Polish, Slavish, Bohemian, Croatian, Macedonian, Bulgarian and Russian."[266] A third man identified himself as a "an interpreter of languages: Bulgarian, Russian, Macedonian, Italian, Greek, Polish, Slavish, Roumanian, Albanian and Turkish."[267] A fourth advertisement was seeking a "correspondent in English, French, Russian, Roumanian, Bulgarian, Macedonian, Servian and Croatian; good experience."[268]

Advertisements listing the Macedonian language is one thing. However, the powerful editorial of a Macedonian woman explaining Macedonians and Bulgarians is another. The following editorial is from October of 1927 by a woman named Kotchova. She wrote:

**I notice in your paper the following headline: 'Jugoslav Break With Bulgaria is Threatened.' I am a pure Macedonian woman by birth and right and have come into this country just recently. Such events as I read in the *Post-Dispatch* are not rare in my country. But what I wish to make clear is that no Bulgarians are causing the trouble. The comitadjis are natives of Macedonia itself who are tired of and dissatisfied with the present regime in Macedonia, or such who have been driven from their homes by force. I wonder why we Macedonians don't take the blame ourselves? We leave the world to think that Bulgaria came into our country (into other people's country) and caused trouble. Why blame somebody for our**

mistakes? The Christian spirit rebels at this and I wish I could make all the world see and know that no Bulgarian has anything to do in Macedonia but we are the ones who revolt. Why? Protogerov is a Macedonian and so are his followers, then why blame others?"[269]

Furthermore, the nationwide pro-Macedonian organization in the United States, the Macedonian People's League (MPL), had a foothold in Granite City, while the pro-Bulgarian Macedonian Political Organization (MPO) was largely rejected by Granite City's Macedonians. For example, in its nearly 100-year history, the MPO never held a convention in Granite City or Madison. They had one in St. Louis in 1942; but St. Louis had a large Bulgarian population. The MPL, however, held its eight convention in Madison in September of 1938. The Madison branch was named the P. Chaulev branch (after a left-wing Macedonian IMRO leader). The league was "composed of Americans of Macedonian birth or descent" and insisted it was seeking support for the national independence movement in Macedonia, which was divided among Yugoslavia, Greece and Bulgaria. "The convention city, Madison, has one of the oldest Macedonian colonies in the United States," said the announcement. "Some of its residents participated in the great Elinden Uprising of August 2, 1903, when the people of Macedonia made an heroic but unsuccessful effort to throw of Turkish domination."[270]

The year before, in November of 1937, it was reported that an MPL member who had lived in Madison was killed in the war in Spain as a member of the Spanish Republicans. Louis Marcovsky used to work in the steel mills in Granite City and then enlisted in the International Brigade supporting the Spanish loyalists. At the time of his death, he was 40 years old.

As a youngster, he fought alongside the Greek Army during the First World War and was decorated for his bravery. He had joined the Spanish loyalist cause out of a firm conviction against global Fascism. He enlisted with the George Dimitroff Battalion. He became an American citizen in Detroit in 1932 after working in Madison throughout the 1920s. He visited Madison in summer of 1937 to say goodbye to his cousins and friends. Word of his death came to his cousin Naum Marcovsky, who was a grocer in Madison, from a cablegram of a comrade who had helped Louis get to the hospital after he was shot. The Madison branch of the Macedonian People's League held a memorial service for him.[271]

Another Macedonian, Tom Kalemoff of St. Louis, arrived at the city hall in the summer of 1942 insisting that he wanted to contribute to the U.S. war effort. The 56-year-old, who was born in Macedonia and had been in St. Louis since 1912, showed four checks drawn against his bank account and $150 in War Stamps. Checks were made out to the Navy, Red Cross, Salvation Army, and City Fund. These were his profits from his soft drink business. "But what's profits," he asked. "If we don't win the war, what good is our money?" He had bought $1,000 in ward bonds in 1941 and wanted to do the same this year. He then produced a pamphlet from the MPL: "Help America and the United Nations win the war and the peace," said the circular. "The United States declaration of war against the Fascist government of Bulgaria will hasten the day of liberation of the Bulgarian and Macedonian peoples from the double yoke of Hitler and King Boris Second and Last." Kalemoff said: "That's the way I feel."[272]

Going back to the early decades of that 20th century, many Macedonian village societies sprouted throughout Granite City and Madison. These associations were a means for people from the same village to assist one another in social, financial and cultural matters. The following is a list of such organizations:

- Bitola Friendship Society, Granite City, 1913
- Smrdesh Friendship Society, Madison, 1906
- Dumbensko Brotherhood, Madison, 1906
- Brznishko Friendship Society, Madison, 1909.
- Kosinsko Friendship Society, Madison, 1906[273]
- Oshchima Friendship Society, Madison, 1907
- Aposkep Society, Madison, 1907
- Setoma Friendship Society, Granite City, 1917
- Potkrepa Mutual Aid Society, Granite City, 1926[274]

Further, other groups that catered to Macedonians and Bulgarians developed in the area, such as the Madison County chapter of the MPO, which was located about 18 miles north of Granite City in Alton.

Moreover, in addition to these several groups, other Macedonian organizations appeared. For example, in February of 1909, three Macedonian men – George D. Popoff, Krste Koloff and Alex Castoff – created the Macedonian Commercial Club of Granite City. Their stated object was to promote the good of the Macedonian community. They set out to achieve this by doing the following tasks: "To buy and sell general merchandise, to run a boardinghouse and dram shop, to be agent for importers, steamboat tickets and foreign exchange, to operate a truck farm and vegetable market."[275] In a way, it was clever branding in order to appeal to the Macedonian community.

There were also Macedonian newspapers other than *Naroden Glas* and *Macedonia*. In 1910, the *Rabotnicheska Prosveta* (Worker's Enlightenment) came into existence. It was a socialist paper that catered to the left-wing Macedonians in Granite City, which was a substantial segment of the Macedonian population. Shortly after that, *Makedonska Glas* was founded, and it heavily espoused the need for a Macedonian revolution to achieve independence for occupied Macedonia. That paper only lasted a few months. Finally, there was another socialist paper called *Narodna Prosveta* (People's Enlightenment), which also only existed for a few issues.[276]

While the Macedonian community in Granite City today is negligible, especially compared to the many other towns and cities that harbor large Macedonian populations, Granite's City legacy as the flame for the Macedonian spirit in America during the early 20$^{th}$ century is uncontested. These Macedonians formed a colony that embodied the spirit of community, culture, identity and intellectual curiosity: over five Macedonian newspapers circulated through Granite City's streets; at least a dozen friendship, cultural and political groups dotted the landscape; cultural events and political activism was not infrequent; and individual Macedonians were unafraid to express their opinion, especially about their Turkish occupiers at first, and later about their Greek and Bulgarian neighbors.

Out of this community arose some of southern Illinois's wealthiest individuals. Just a handful of men accumulated a combined net-worth equivalent to tens of millions of dollars in today's value. These men created the necessary infrastructure and provided the desired amenities for a Macedonian colony to thrive: boarding houses, grocers, saloons, bakeries, meat shops, labor agencies, steamship agencies, and banks. The common Macedonian – although only fleetingly in Granite City – helped build America through their cheap labor and helped rebuild their villages in Macedonia with the small fortunes that they amassed.

The first Macedonian colony in America no longer exists, but its legacy will be imprinted in the minds of Macedonians and Macedonian-Americans forever. While the Macedonian's roots are firmly planted in Macedonia, the Macedonian's spirit flourishes in America because of the efforts and contributions of Granite City's original Macedonians. The history of the Macedonian people is incomplete without an appreciation of this first Macedonian colony.

# ENDNOTES

[1] Solun was a part of Macedonia until its division in 1913. Currently, Solun is in northern Greece, or Aegean Macedonia. It is widely known as Thessaloniki or Salonica. Throughout this book, Macedonian names for towns and cities will be used, whether or not that place is located in Macedonia, Greece or Bulgaria.

[2] Anastasoff, Christ, *The Tragic Peninsula*, 1935, 56-62.

[3] "The True History of the Macedonian Rising", *Black & White, Vol. 26*, (H.S. Wood, London: 1903), Pg. 388.

[4] MacDermott, MacDermott, *For freedom and perfection: a biography of Jane Sandanski*, (1987), 61.

[5] "The Macedonian Agitation", *The Times*, London, April 12, 1901,. 3-4

[6] MacDermott, MacDermott, *For freedom and perfection: a biography of Jane Sandanski*, (1987), 223.

[7] Smith, Arthur D.H., *Fighting the Turk in the Balkans: An American's Adventures with the Macedonian Revolutionists*, (New York: G.P. Putnam's Sons, 1908), Pg. 28.

[8] Mary Edith Durham, *The Burden of the Balkans*, (Edward Arnold, London, 1904), 113.

[9] MacDermott, MacDermott, *For freedom and perfection: a biography of Jane Sandanski*, (1987), 219, 220.

[10] Sinadinoski, Victor, *The Macedonian Resurrection: The Story of the Internal Macedonian Revolutionary Organization*, (Burlington, 2017), Pg. 71.

[11] Krste Bitkovski, "Macedonia in the XIX Century," in Todor Chepreganov, ed., *History of the Macedonian People*, (Institute of National History, 2008), 187.

[12] Anastasoff, Christ, *The Tragic Peninsula*, 1935, 61.

[13] "A Terrible Threat", *St. John Daily*, Sun, Jun. 9, 1903, 6.

[14] "Greeks Tremble at Coming of a U.S. Inspector," *St. Louis Post-Dispatch* (St. Louis, Missouri) · Sun, Jan 26, 1908 · Page 16

[15] Petras, Ronald, "Lincoln Place: In Honor of a President," (Granite City, Illinois), 2012, Pg. 1.

[16] Cassens, David E., "The Bulgarian Colony of Southwestern Illinois, 1900-1920," *Illinois Historical Journal, Vol. 84*, (Spring 1991).

[17] "5 Bulgarians Held in Greek Shooting Case," St. Louis Post-Dispatch (St. Louis, Missouri) · Sat, Jun 29, 1907 · Page 3; "Police of Middle West Now Confronted by Problem as Perplexing as Mafia", St. Louis Post-Dispatch (St. Louis, Missouri), Sep 1, 1907, Page 50

[18] "Slain Bandit Chief had Followers on East Side," St. Louis Post-Dispatch (St. Louis, Missouri), Dec 15, 1907, Page 28

[19] "Greeks Tremble at Coming of a U.S. Inspector," St. Louis Post-Dispatch (St. Louis, Missouri) · Sun, Jan 26, 1908 · Page 16

[20] "Getting the War News," St. Louis Post-Dispatch (St. Louis, Missouri), Feb 9, 1913, Page 50; "Greeks Tremble at Coming of a U.S. Inspector," St. Louis Post-Dispatch (St. Louis, Missouri) · Sun, Jan 26, 1908 · Page 16
[21] The newspaper was in the Bulgarian language as Macedonian did not exist as an officially codified language.
[22] "Slain Bandit Chief had Followers on East Side," St. Louis Post-Dispatch (St. Louis, Missouri), Dec 15, 1907, Page 28
[23] Smith, Arthur D.H., *Fighting the Turk in the Balkans: An American's Adventures with the Macedonian Revolutionists*, (New York: G.P. Putnam's Sons, 1908), Pg. 30.
[24] Eleanor Hulda Calhoun Lazarovich-Hrebelianovich, *Pleasures and Palaces: The Memoirs of Princess Lazarovich-Hrebelianovich*, The Century Co., New York, 1915, Pg. 335-338.
[25] Frederick Moore, "Bulgarian Brigand Sandansky Sides with Young Turks in Their Fight for Freedom," *The Washington Post* (Washington, District of Columbia) 30 Aug 1908, Sun Page 3
[26] "The Murder of Sarafoff," *The Guardian* (London, Greater London, England) 17 Dec 1907, Tue Page 7
[27] "Macedonian Cockpit," *The Times* (London, Greater London, England) 25 Feb 1908, Tue Page 5
[28] The Macedonian Orthodox Church did not obtain independence until the 1960s.
[29] "Slain Bandit Chief had Followers on East Side," St. Louis Post-Dispatch (St. Louis, Missouri), Dec 15, 1907, Page 28
[30] "Start Riot Over Alleged Insult," *Alton Evening Telegraph* (Alton, Illinois), Feb 15, 1909, Page 3
[31] "Start Riot Over Alleged Insult," *Alton Evening Telegraph* (Alton, Illinois), Feb 15, 1909, Page 3
[32] "Start Riot Over Alleged Insult," *Alton Evening Telegraph* (Alton, Illinois), Feb 15, 1909, Page 3
[33] "Start Riot Over Alleged Insult," *Alton Evening Telegraph* (Alton, Illinois), Feb 15, 1909, Page 3
[34] "Start Riot Over Alleged Insult," *Alton Evening Telegraph* (Alton, Illinois), Feb 15, 1909, Page 3
[35] St. Louis Post-Dispatch (St. Louis, Missouri) · Sun, Mar 3, 1907 · Page 56
[36] Demetre's Story," The Public Ledger (Maysville, Kentucky) 19 Apr 1907, Fri Page 3
[37] "Black Hand Falls in Path of Police," The Indianapolis Star (Indianapolis, Indiana) 28 Dec 1906, Fri Page 3
[38] Ed. John Boardman and N.G.L. Hammond, The Cambridge Ancient History, Volume 3, Part 3, (Cambridge: Cambridge University Press, 1982), Pg. 280.
[39] William Smith, Dictionary of Greek and Roman Geography (1854), http://www.perseus.tufts.edu/hopper/text?doc=Perseus%3Atext%3A1999.04.00

64%3Aalphabetic+letter%3DC%3Aentry+group%3D23%3Aentry%3Dcrestonia-geo . Last accessed 1.31.2019.

[40] Kukush is located in Aegean Macedonia, in northern Greece, about 30 miles north of Thessaloniki.

[41] "Blackmail and Plot to Murder Revealed," The Inter Ocean (Chicago, Illinois) · Sun, Dec 16, 1906 · Page 10

[42] St. Louis Post-Dispatch (St. Louis, Missouri) · Sun, Mar 3, 1907 · Page 56

[43] "After Bulgarian Black Hand," Woodford County Journal (Eureka, Illinois) · Thu, Dec 6, 1906 · Page 3

[44] "Black Hand Levies on Danville Greeks," The Decatur Herald (Decatur, Illinois) 23 Nov 1906, Fri Page 3

[45] "Bulgarians Released on Bond Over Protests," The Indianapolis News (Indianapolis, Indiana) · Tue, Dec 18, 1906 · Page 11

[46] "Levy Blackmail on the Greeks," The Akron Beacon Journal (Akron, Ohio) 15 Dec 1906, Sat Page 1

[47] St. Louis Post-Dispatch (St. Louis, Missouri) · Sun, Mar 3, 1907 · Page 56

[48] "Blackmail and Plot to Murder Revealed," The Inter Ocean (Chicago, Illinois) · Sun, Dec 16, 1906 · Page 10

[49] "Blackmail and Plot to Murder Revealed," The Inter Ocean (Chicago, Illinois) · Sun, Dec 16, 1906 · Page 10

[50] "11 Arrests for Black Hand Crime," St. Louis Post-Dispatch (St. Louis, Missouri) · Thu, Mar 29, 1906 · Page 10

[51] "11 Arrests for Black Hand Crime," St. Louis Post-Dispatch (St. Louis, Missouri) · Thu, Mar 29, 1906 · Page 10

[52] "New Clue", Star Tribune (Minneapolis, Minnesota) · Sun, Apr 1, 1906 · Page 1, 2.

[53] "City's Worst Murder Still Unsolved", Star Tribune (Minneapolis, Minnesota) 22 Dec 1940, Sun Page 13

[54] "Does Death Mean Bandit's Revenge?", The Minneapolis Journal (Minneapolis, Minnesota)20 Oct 1906, Sat Page 1; "Body at Morgue is Still Unidentified", The Minneapolis Journal (Minneapolis, Minnesota)21 Oct 1906, Sun Page 6.

[55] "City's Worst Murder Still Unsolved", Star Tribune (Minneapolis, Minnesota)22 Dec 1940, Sun Page 13

[56] "Urged," The Cincinnati Enquirer (Cincinnati, Ohio) · Fri, Jul 26, 1907 · Page 12; The Public Ledger (Maysville, Kentucky) 27 Jul 1907, Sat Page 3

[57] "Murderer Captured," The Public Ledger (Maysville, Kentucky) 15 Apr 1907, Mon Page 1

[58] "Black Hand," The Public Ledger (Maysville, Kentucky) 07 Jun 1907, Fri Page 1

[59] "Demetre's Story," The Public Ledger (Maysville, Kentucky) 19 Apr 1907, Fri Page 3

[60] St. Louis Post-Dispatch (St. Louis, Missouri) · Sun, Mar 3, 1907 · Page 56

[61] St. Louis Post-Dispatch (St. Louis, Missouri) · Sun, Mar 3, 1907 · Page 56

[62] "Balkan Wars are Revived in St. Louis," St. Louis Post-Dispatch (St. Louis, Missouri) · Tue, Nov 27, 1906 · Page 2

[63] "Balkan Wars are Revived in St. Louis," St. Louis Post-Dispatch (St. Louis, Missouri) · Tue, Nov 27, 1906 · Page 2

[64] "Bulgarian Accused of Conspiracy," The Indianapolis News (Indianapolis, Indiana) · Sat, Nov 24, 1906 · Page 21

[65] St. Louis Post-Dispatch (St. Louis, Missouri) · Sun, Mar 3, 1907 · Page 56

[66] "Blackmail and Plot to Murder Revealed," The Inter Ocean (Chicago, Illinois) · Sun, Dec 16, 1906 · Page 10

[67] "Black Hand Falls in Path of Police," The Indianapolis Star (Indianapolis, Indiana) 28 Dec 1906, Fri Page 3

[68] "Black Hand Levies on Danville Greeks," The Decatur Herald (Decatur, Illinois) 23 Nov 1906, Fri Page 3

[69] "Black Hand Falls in Path of Police," The Indianapolis Star (Indianapolis, Indiana) 28 Dec 1906, Fri Page 3

[70] The Greek consuls insisted the victims were Greeks because they were a part of the Greek church. The victims referred to themselves as Macedonians and did not speak Greek that well. At the trial, it was shown that they did not speak Greek as well as Bulgarian or Macedonians.

[71] "Black Hand Falls in Path of Police," The Indianapolis Star (Indianapolis, Indiana) 28 Dec 1906, Fri Page 3

[72] There does not seem to be evidence that Macedonian agents were involved in her assassination.

[73] "Black Hand Levies on Danville Greeks," The Decatur Herald (Decatur, Illinois) 23 Nov 1906, Fri Page 3

[74] "Blackmail and Plot to Murder Revealed," The Inter Ocean (Chicago, Illinois) · Sun, Dec 16, 1906 · Page 10

[75] "Levy Blackmail on the Greeks," The Akron Beacon Journal (Akron, Ohio) 15 Dec 1906, Sat Page 1

[76] The Greeks sometimes referred to them as Bulgarians, sometimes as Macedonians, and sometimes as both.

[77] "War on Blackmailers," Evening Star (Washington, District of Columbia) · Fri, Dec 28, 1906 · Page 1

[78] Shoomkoff uses Roucheff. I substituted Roucheff for Roumaneff to remain consistent.

[79] "Says Greeks are Seeking Revenge on Foreigners," The Indianapolis News (Indianapolis, Indiana) 23 Feb 1907, Sat Page 3

[80] "Blackmail Plot is Revealed," The La Crosse Tribune (La Crosse, Wisconsin) 15 Mar 1907, Fri Page 11

[81] Roumaneff is substituted for Roucheff, as the original author wrote, for consistency.

[82] "Greece vs. Bulgaria," The Indianapolis Star (Indianapolis, Indiana) · Wed, Jan 23, 1907 · Page 8

[83] "Sofia Society a Myth," The Indianapolis Star (Indianapolis, Indiana) · Sun, Feb 24, 1907 · Page 16
[84] "Devotion of Minister Likely to Win Reward," The Indianapolis Star (Indianapolis, Indiana) 09 Jun 1907, Sun Page 16
[85] "Strife of Tongues to Air Conspiracy," The Indianapolis Star (Indianapolis, Indiana) 07 Mar 1907, Thu Page 5
[86] "Found Guilty of Blackmail," The Indianapolis Star (Indianapolis, Indiana) · Wed, Dec 19, 1906 · Page 6
[87] "Found Guilty of Blackmail," The Indianapolis Star (Indianapolis, Indiana) · Wed, Dec 19, 1906 · Page 6
[88] "Bulgarians Released on Bond Over Protests," The Indianapolis News (Indianapolis, Indiana) · Tue, Dec 18, 1906 · Page 11
[89] "Bulgarians found Guilty," The Richmond Item (Richmond, Indiana) · Wed, Mar 13, 1907 · Page 5
[90] "Blackmail Plot is Revealed," The La Crosse Tribune (La Crosse, Wisconsin) 15 Mar 1907, Fri Page 11
[91] "Bulgarians are Released," The Indianapolis Star (Indianapolis, Indiana) 10 May 1907, Page 15
[92] Police of Middle West Now Confronted by Problem as Perplexing as Mafia", St. Louis Post-Dispatch (St. Louis, Missouri), Sep 1, 1907, Page 50
[93] "Police of Middle West Now Confronted by Problem as Perplexing as Mafia", St. Louis Post-Dispatch (St. Louis, Missouri), Sep 1, 1907, Page 50
[94] Police of Middle West Now Confronted by Problem as Perplexing as Mafia", St. Louis Post-Dispatch (St. Louis, Missouri), Sep 1, 1907, Page 50
[95] "5 Bulgarians Held in Greek Shooting Case," St. Louis Post-Dispatch (St. Louis, Missouri) · Sat, Jun 29, 1907 · Page 3
[96] Police of Middle West Now Confronted by Problem as Perplexing as Mafia", St. Louis Post-Dispatch (St. Louis, Missouri), Sep 1, 1907, Page 50
[97] The Greeks often referred to all Slavic-speaking Macedonians as Bulgarians. To this day, the Greeks do not recognize the ethnic Macedonian identity or Macedonian language.
[98] "5 Bulgarians Held in Greek Shooting Case," St. Louis Post-Dispatch (St. Louis, Missouri) · Sat, Jun 29, 1907 · Page 3
[99] Police of Middle West Now Confronted by Problem as Perplexing as Mafia", St. Louis Post-Dispatch (St. Louis, Missouri), Sep 1, 1907, Page 50
[100] Police of Middle West Now Confronted by Problem as Perplexing as Mafia", St. Louis Post-Dispatch (St. Louis, Missouri), Sep 1, 1907, Page 50
[101] "5 Bulgarians Held in Greek Shooting Case," St. Louis Post-Dispatch (St. Louis, Missouri) · Sat, Jun 29, 1907 · Page 3
[102] "Greeks Tremble at Coming of a U.S. Inspector," St. Louis Post-Dispatch (St. Louis, Missouri) · Sun, Jan 26, 1908 · Page 16
[103] "Feuds of Greek and Bulgarian Rend Tri-Cities," St. Louis Post-Dispatch (St. Louis, Missouri) · Sun, Aug 4, 1907 · Page 43

[104] "Police of Middle West Now Confronted by Problem as Perplexing as Mafia", St. Louis Post-Dispatch (St. Louis, Missouri), Sep 1, 1907, Page 50

[105] "Feuds of Greek and Bulgarian Rend Tri-Cities," St. Louis Post-Dispatch (St. Louis, Missouri) · Sun, Aug 4, 1907 · Page 43

[106] "Police of Middle West Now Confronted by Problem as Perplexing as Mafia", St. Louis Post-Dispatch (St. Louis, Missouri), Sep 1, 1907, Page 50

[107] "Hungry Hollow Race Riots Puts Three in Bed," St. Louis Post-Dispatch (St. Louis, Missouri) 10 Aug 1907, Sat Page 2

[108] "Hungry Hollow Race Riots Puts Three in Bed," St. Louis Post-Dispatch (St. Louis, Missouri) 10 Aug 1907, Sat Page 2

[109] "Post-Dispatch is Threatened by Black Hand," St. Louis Post-Dispatch (St. Louis, Missouri) · Sat, Jul 27, 1907 · Page 2

[110] "Urged," The Cincinnati Enquirer (Cincinnati, Ohio) · Fri, Jul 26, 1907 · Page 12

[111] "Black Hand Men Flee When Tryst is Kept," St. Louis Post-Dispatch (St. Louis, Missouri), Oct 13, 1907, Page 25

[112] "Black Hand Men Flee When Tryst is Kept," St. Louis Post-Dispatch (St. Louis, Missouri), Oct 13, 1907, Page 25

[113] "Black Hand Men Flee When Tryst is Kept," St. Louis Post-Dispatch (St. Louis, Missouri), Oct 13, 1907, Page 25

[114] "Rich Greek is Warned by Black Hand," St. Louis Post-Dispatch (St. Louis, Missouri) · Sun, Mar 1, 1908 · Page 24

[115] "Greeks Tremble at Coming of a U.S. Inspector," St. Louis Post-Dispatch (St. Louis, Missouri) · Sun, Jan 26, 1908 · Page 16

[116] "Greeks Tremble at Coming of a U.S. Inspector," St. Louis Post-Dispatch (St. Louis, Missouri) · Sun, Jan 26, 1908 · Page 16

[117] "Greeks Tremble at Coming of a U.S. Inspector," St. Louis Post-Dispatch (St. Louis, Missouri) · Sun, Jan 26, 1908 · Page 16

[118] Petras, Ronald, "Lincoln Place: In Honor of a President," (Granite City, Illinois), 2012, Pg. 1.

[119] Ed. Stephanoff, Vasil and Grammaticoff, Vasil, "Bulgarian-American Almanac for 1922," (Granite City: Naroden Glas, 1922), Pg. 82.

[120] "Former Banker Denies Taking Part in Plot," The Edwardsville Intelligencer (Edwardsville, Illinois) · Mon, Sep 25, 1933 · Page 1

[121] Ed. Stephanoff, Vasil and Grammaticoff, Vasil, "Bulgarian-American Almanac for 1922," (Granite City: Naroden Glas, 1922), Pg. 82.

[122] "Bulgarian-American Calendar-Almanac for 1920," (Granite City: Naroden Glas, 1920), Pg. 161.

[123] "United States World War I Draft Registration Cards, 1917-1918," database with images, *FamilySearch* (https://familysearch.org/ark:/61903/1:1:K6D5-YCD : 13 March 2018), Nicholas Alabach, 1917-1918; citing Madison County no 3, Illinois, United States, NARA microfilm publication M1509 (Washington D.C.: National Archives and Records Administration, n.d.); FHL microfilm 1,614,328.

[124] "United States Census, 1920," database with images, *FamilySearch* (https://familysearch.org/ark:/61903/1:1:MJHF-SMG : accessed 3 February 2019), Nick Alabach, Granite Ward 5, Madison, Illinois, United States; citing ED 85, sheet 3A, line 29, family 60, NARA microfilm publication T625 (Washington D.C.: National Archives and Records Administration, 1992), roll 390; FHL microfilm 1,820,390.

[125] "Bulgarian-American Calendar-Almanac for 1920," (Granite City: Naroden Glas, 1920), Pg. 161.

[126] St. Louis Post-Dispatch (St. Louis, Missouri) 07 Apr 1909, Wed Page 14

[127] St. Louis Post-Dispatch (St. Louis, Missouri) 31 Mar 1909, Wed Page 4

[128] "United States Census, 1920," database with images, *FamilySearch* (https://familysearch.org/ark:/61903/1:1:MJHF-SMG : accessed 3 February 2019), Nick Alabach, Granite Ward 5, Madison, Illinois, United States; citing ED 85, sheet 3A, line 29, family 60, NARA microfilm publication T625 (Washington D.C.: National Archives and Records Administration, 1992), roll 390; FHL microfilm 1,820,390.

[129] "Bulgarians in a Feud," The Edwardsville Intelligencer (Edwardsville, Illinois) · Fri, Jun 26, 1908 · Page 8

[130] "Bulgarian Banks are Born in Granite City," The Indianapolis News (Indianapolis, Indiana) · Sat, May 30, 1908 · Page 10

[131] "Bulgarian Banks are Born in Granite City," The Indianapolis News (Indianapolis, Indiana) · Sat, May 30, 1908 · Page 10

[132] "Fine of $3 is Levied in Feud of Macedonians," St. Louis Post-Dispatch (St. Louis, Missouri) · Wed, Aug 4, 1909 · Page 14

[133] "Doctor Sues Bulgarian Editor," St. Louis Post-Dispatch (St. Louis, Missouri) · Sun, Dec 8, 1907 · Page 36

[134] "Stung the Editor," The Edwardsville Intelligencer (Edwardsville, Illinois) · Thu, Feb 27, 1908 · Page 1

[135] "Monthly Bath is Fatal," Alton Evening Telegraph (Alton, Illinois) · Mon, Jul 25, 1910 · Page 3

[136] "Melting Pot Proposed," The Springfield News-Leader (Springfield, Missouri) · Thu, Mar 4, 1915 · Page 5

[137] Petras, Ronald, "Lincoln Place: In Honor of a President," (Granite City, Illinois), 2012, Pg. 1.

[138] Petras, Ronald, "Lincoln Place: In Honor of a President," (Granite City, Illinois), 2012, Pg. 3.

[139] Petras, Ronald, "Lincoln Place: In Honor of a President," (Granite City, Illinois), 2012, Pg. 19.

[140] "Illinois Deaths and Stillbirths, 1916-1947," database, *FamilySearch* (https://familysearch.org/ark:/61903/1:1:N3XQ-K7J : 8 March 2018), Kosla A. Mitsareff, 02 Feb 1918; Public Board of Health, Archives, Springfield; FHL microfilm 1,544,187.

[141] "New Macedonia," Alton Evening Telegraph, Alton, Madison, Illinois. Wed, Dec 19, 1906 · Page 3
[142] "Unsolicited Testimonial," St. Louis Post-Dispatch (St. Louis, Missouri) 22 Feb 1908, Sat Page 10
[143] "New Macedonia," Alton Evening Telegraph, Alton, Madison, Illinois. Wed, Dec 19, 1906 · Page 3
[144] "Killing in Granite City," Alton Evening Telegraph (Alton, Illinois) 22 Mar 1911, Wed Page 6
[145] "Bulgarian Banks are Born in Granite City," The Indianapolis News (Indianapolis, Indiana) · Sat, May 30, 1908 · Page 10
[146] "Bulgarian Banks are Born in Granite City," The Indianapolis News (Indianapolis, Indiana) · Sat, May 30, 1908 · Page 10
[147] "Bulgarian Banks are Born in Granite City," The Indianapolis News (Indianapolis, Indiana) · Sat, May 30, 1908 · Page 10
[148] "Bulgarian Banks are Born in Granite City," The Indianapolis News (Indianapolis, Indiana) · Sat, May 30, 1908 · Page 10
[149] "Black Hand Men Flee When Tryst is Kept," St. Louis Post-Dispatch (St. Louis, Missouri), Oct 13, 1907, Page 25
[150] "Financial King Accuses Partner of $35,000 Theft," St. Louis Post-Dispatch (St. Louis, Missouri), Jun 16, 1909, Page 3
[151] "Exiled County Kills Partner," The St. Louis Star and Times (St. Louis, Missouri) · Wed, Mar 22, 1911 · Page 12; "Brother-In-Law He Evicted Kills Bulgarian King," St. Louis Post-Dispatch (St. Louis, Missouri), Mar 22, 1911, Page 2
[152] "Accident Kills Rich Turk," The St. Anne Record, St. Anne, Illinois, Mar 12, 1909, Pg.
[153] "Financial King Accuses Partner of $35,000 Theft," St. Louis Post-Dispatch (St. Louis, Missouri), Jun 16, 1909, Page 3; "Brother-In-Law He Evicted Kills Bulgarian King," St. Louis Post-Dispatch (St. Louis, Missouri), Mar 22, 1911, Page 2
[154] "Financial King Accuses Partner of $35,000 Theft," St. Louis Post-Dispatch (St. Louis, Missouri), Jun 16, 1909, Page 3
[155] "Financial King Accuses Partner of $35,000 Theft," St. Louis Post-Dispatch (St. Louis, Missouri), Jun 16, 1909, Page 3
[156] "Financial King Accuses Partner of $35,000 Theft," St. Louis Post-Dispatch (St. Louis, Missouri), Jun 16, 1909, Page 3
[157] "Deputy Sheriff Makes a Long Trip for Prisoner," The Edwardsville Intelligencer (Edwardsville, Illinois) 25 Jun 1909, Fri Page 8
[158] "Some Brief Paragraphs," The Edwardsville Intelligencer (Edwardsville, Illinois) 28 Jun 1909, Mon Page 4
[159] "Financial King Accuses Partner of $35,000 Theft," St. Louis Post-Dispatch (St. Louis, Missouri), Jun 16, 1909, Page 3
[160] "Banker Under Charges," The Edwardsville Intelligencer (Edwardsville, Illinois) · Fri, Apr 30, 1909, Page 1

[161] "Banker Under Charges," The Edwardsville Intelligencer (Edwardsville, Illinois) · Fri, Apr 30, 1909, Page 1
[162] "Embezzlement Charge Against Labor Banker," St. Louis Post-Dispatch (St. Louis, Missouri) · Sat, May 1, 1909 · Page 3
[163] "Embezzlement Charge Against Labor Banker," St. Louis Post-Dispatch (St. Louis, Missouri) · Sat, May 1, 1909 · Page 3
[164] "Exiled County Kills Partner," The St. Louis Star and Times (St. Louis, Missouri) · Wed, Mar 22, 1911 · Page 12
[165] "Killing in Granite City,"    Alton Evening Telegraph (Alton, Illinois) 22 Mar 1911, Wed Page 6
[166] "Brother-In-Law He Evicted Kills Bulgarian King," St. Louis Post-Dispatch (St. Louis, Missouri), Mar 22, 1911, Page 2
[167] "Exiled County Kills Partner," The St. Louis Star and Times (St. Louis, Missouri) · Wed, Mar 22, 1911 · Page 12
[168] "Brother-In-Law He Evicted Kills Bulgarian King," St. Louis Post-Dispatch (St. Louis, Missouri), Mar 22, 1911, Page 2
[169] "Brother-In-Law He Evicted Kills Bulgarian King," St. Louis Post-Dispatch (St. Louis, Missouri), Mar 22, 1911, Page 2
[170] "Brother-In-Law He Evicted Kills Bulgarian King," St. Louis Post-Dispatch (St. Louis, Missouri), Mar 22, 1911, Page 2
[171] "Exiled County Kills Partner," The St. Louis Star and Times (St. Louis, Missouri) · Wed, Mar 22, 1911 · Page 12
[172] "Woman Testifies She Saw Brother Kill Her Husband," St. Louis Post-Dispatch (St. Louis, Missouri), Nov 6, 1911, Page 3
[173] "Christmas Gift Death Agency," Alton Evening Telegraph (Alton, Illinois) 24 Mar 1911, Fri Page 7
[174] "Man Fatally Shot by Realty Dealer in Business Feud,"    St. Louis Post-Dispatch (St. Louis, Missouri)  03 Feb 1918, Sun  Page 28
[175] "Man Shot by Realty Dealer in Quarrel," St. Louis Post-Dispatch (St. Louis, Missour), Feb 2, 1918; "Morris is Exonerated in Killing of Mitsareff," St. Louis Post-Dispatch (St. Louis, Missouri) · Tue, Feb 5, 1918 · Page 15
[176] "Abstracts of Reports of the Immigration Commission: Vol. 1, Presented by Mr. Dillingham, (Washington: Government Printing Office, 1911), Pg. 496.
[177] "To Teach Countrymen," The Edwardsville Intelligencer (Edwardsville, Illinois) · Tue, Oct 6, 1908 · Page 1
[178] "Greeks Tremble at Coming of a U.S. Inspector," St. Louis Post-Dispatch (St. Louis, Missouri) · Sun, Jan 26, 1908 · Page 16
[179] "Bulgarian-American Calendar-Almanac for 1920," (Granite City: Naroden Glas, 1920), Pg. 174-175.
[180] "Young Sophomore at Washington U. Out for Congress," The St. Louis Star and Times (St. Louis, Missouri) · Fri, Jul 11, 1924 · Page 5
[181] The St. Louis Star and Times (St. Louis, Missouri) · Mon, Nov 1, 1926 · Page 17

[182] Putzel, Max, "Once a Leader in the Balkan Wars, Now a Pacifist," St. Louis Post-Dispatch (St. Louis, Missouri) · Sun, Nov 18, 1934 · Page 63

[183] Putzel, Max, "Once a Leader in the Balkan Wars, Now a Pacifist," St. Louis Post-Dispatch (St. Louis, Missouri) · Sun, Nov 18, 1934 · Page 63

[184] Putzel, Max, "Once a Leader in the Balkan Wars, Now a Pacifist," St. Louis Post-Dispatch (St. Louis, Missouri) · Sun, Nov 18, 1934 · Page 63

[185] "Granite City Alien Tells Court How He Would Run U.S.," The St. Louis Star and Times (St. Louis, Missouri) · Sat, Mar 5, 1932 · Page 3

[186] Christowe, Stoyan, The Eagle and the Stork, (New York: Harper's Magazin, 1976), Pg. 160-161.

[187] "Bulgarian-American Calendar-Almanac for 1920," (Granite City: Naroden Glas, 1920), Pg. 161.

[188] "Bulgarian-American Calendar-Almanac for 1920," (Granite City: Naroden Glas, 1920), Pg. 165.

[189] "Bulgarian-American Calendar-Almanac for 1920," (Granite City: Naroden Glas, 1920), Pg. 168.

[190] "Bulgarian-American Calendar-Almanac for 1920," (Granite City: Naroden Glas, 1920), Pg. 169.

[191] "Bulgarian-American Calendar-Almanac for 1920," (Granite City: Naroden Glas, 1920), Pg. 176.

[192] "Bulgarian-American Calendar-Almanac for 1920," (Granite City: Naroden Glas, 1920), Pg. 177.

[193] "Bulgarian-American Calendar-Almanac for 1920," (Granite City: Naroden Glas, 1920), Pg. 177.

[194] "Bulgarian-American Calendar-Almanac for 1920," (Granite City: Naroden Glas, 1920), Pg. 179.

[195] "Bulgarian-American Calendar-Almanac for 1920," (Granite City: Naroden Glas, 1920), Pg. 180.

[196] "White Cheese Factory," The Edwardsville Intelligencer (Edwardsville, Illinois) · Wed, Jun 4, 1919 · Page 1

[197] Ed. Stephanoff, Vasil and Grammaticoff, Vasil, "Bulgarian-American Almanac for 1922," (Granite City: Naroden Glas, 1922), Pg. 79.

[198] Ed. Stephanoff, Vasil and Grammaticoff, Vasil, "Bulgarian-American Almanac for 1922," (Granite City: Naroden Glas, 1922), Pg. 80.

[199] Ed. Stephanoff, Vasil and Grammaticoff, Vasil, "Bulgarian-American Almanac for 1922," (Granite City: Naroden Glas, 1922), Pg. 81.

[200] Ed. Stephanoff, Vasil and Grammaticoff, Vasil, "Bulgarian-American Almanac for 1922," (Granite City: Naroden Glas, 1922), Pg. 83.

[201] Ed. Stephanoff, Vasil and Grammaticoff, Vasil, "Bulgarian-American Almanac for 1922," (Granite City: Naroden Glas, 1922), Pg. 87.

[202] Ed. Stephanoff, Vasil and Grammaticoff, Vasil, "Bulgarian-American Almanac for 1922," (Granite City: Naroden Glas, 1922), Pg. 88.

[203] Ed. Stephanoff, Vasil and Grammaticoff, Vasil, "Bulgarian-American Almanac for 1922," (Granite City: Naroden Glas, 1922), Pg. 89.
[204] Ed. Stephanoff, Vasil and Grammaticoff, Vasil, "Bulgarian-American Almanac for 1922," (Granite City: Naroden Glas, 1922), Pg. 92.
[205] Ed. Stephanoff, Vasil and Grammaticoff, Vasil, "Bulgarian-American Almanac for 1922," (Granite City: Naroden Glas, 1922), Pg. 94.
[206] Ed. Stephanoff, Vasil and Grammaticoff, Vasil, "Bulgarian-American Almanac for 1922," (Granite City: Naroden Glas, 1922), Pg. 95.
[207] Ed. Stephanoff, Vasil and Grammaticoff, Vasil, "Bulgarian-American Almanac for 1922," (Granite City: Naroden Glas, 1922), Pg. 113.
[208] Christowe, Stoyan, The Eagle and the Stork, (New York: Harper's Magazin, 1976), Pg. 172-173, 175.
[209] Christowe, Stoyan, The Eagle and the Stork, (New York: Harper's Magazin, 1976), Pg. 184.
[210] Christowe, Stoyan, The Eagle and the Stork, (New York: Harper's Magazin, 1976), Pg. 186.
[211] Christowe, Stoyan, The Eagle and the Stork, (New York: Harper's Magazin, 1976), Pg. 150.
[212] "Foundry Foreman on Trial for Selling Jobs," St. Louis Post-Dispatch (St. Louis, Missouri) · Mon, Oct 5, 1914 · Page 15
[213] "Adrift Without Work, Man Tells of Hardships," St. Louis Post-Dispatch (St. Louis, Missouri) · Tue, Jul 14, 1908 · Page 2
[214] "Adrift Without Work, Man Tells of Hardships," St. Louis Post-Dispatch (St. Louis, Missouri) · Tue, Jul 14, 1908 · Page 2
[215] "Adrift Without Work, Man Tells of Hardships," St. Louis Post-Dispatch (St. Louis, Missouri) · Tue, Jul 14, 1908 · Page 2
[216] "Adrift Without Work, Man Tells of Hardships," St. Louis Post-Dispatch (St. Louis, Missouri) · Tue, Jul 14, 1908 · Page 2
[217] "Two Hundred Foreigners Are on Strike at Granite," The Edwardsville Intelligencer (Edwardsville, Illinois) · Mon, Mar 15, 1909 · Page 1
[218] "County Cullings," Alton Evening Telegraph (Alton, Illinois) · Tue, Jun 26, 1917 · Page 4; "Drafted into Army," The Edwardsville Intelligencer (Edwardsville, Illinois) · Thu, Feb 24, 1916 · Page 3
[219] "County Cullings," Alton Evening Telegraph (Alton, Illinois) · Tue, Jun 26, 1917 · Page 4; "Drafted into Army," The Edwardsville Intelligencer (Edwardsville, Illinois) · Thu, Feb 24, 1916 · Page 3
[220] The Daily Herald (Arlington Heights, Illinois) · Fri, Apr 24, 1908 · Page 3
[221] "Churches to Aid Hungry Host in the Tri-Cities," St. Louis Post-Dispatch (St. Louis, Missouri) · Mon, May 4, 1908 · Page 4
[222] "Work, Not Confidence," St. Louis Post-Dispatch (St. Louis, Missouri) · Sat, May 9, 1908 · Page 4
[223] "Extra Police to Prevent Rioting," St. Louis Post-Dispatch (St. Louis, Missouri) · Mon, Sep 17, 1906 · Page 3

[224] "Extra Police to Prevent Rioting," St. Louis Post-Dispatch (St. Louis, Missouri) · Mon, Sep 17, 1906 · Page 3; The Daily Herald (Chicago, Illinois) · Fri, Sep 28, 1906 · Page 3; "Race War at Granite City," Alton Evening Telegraph (Alton, Illinois) · Mon, Sep 17, 1906 · Page 3

[225] "Extra Police to Prevent Rioting," St. Louis Post-Dispatch (St. Louis, Missouri) · Mon, Sep 17, 1906 · Page 3; The Daily Herald (Chicago, Illinois) · Fri, Sep 28, 1906 · Page 3; "Race War at Granite City," Alton Evening Telegraph (Alton, Illinois) · Mon, Sep 17, 1906 · Page 3

[226] Cassens, David E., "The Bulgarian Colony of Southwestern Illinois, 1900-1920," *Illinois Historical Journal, Vol. 84*, (Spring 1991).

[227] Petras, Ronald, "Lincoln Place: In Honor of a President," (Granite City, Illinois), 2012, Pg. 1.

[228] Christowe, Stoyan, The Eagle and the Stork, (New York: Harper's Magazin, 1976), Pg. 146-147.

[229] "Leader Pays Fines of Moneyless Europeans," St. Louis Post-Dispatch (St. Louis, Missouri) · Fri, Jun 7, 1907 · Page 10

[230] "Unclean Bakeries Menace Thousands," St. Louis Post-Dispatch (St. Louis, Missouri) · Wed, Feb 12, 1908 · Page 1, 6

[231] "Unclean Bakeries Menace Thousands," St. Louis Post-Dispatch (St. Louis, Missouri) · Wed, Feb 12, 1908 · Page 1, 6

[232] "Raiders Will Stamp Out Bakeshop Menace at Once," St. Louis Post-Dispatch (St. Louis, Missouri) · Thu, Feb 13, 1908 · Page 9

[233] "Council Will Reconsider the Bakeries Bill," St. Louis Post-Dispatch (St. Louis, Missouri) · Fri, Mar 27, 1908 · Page 16

[234] "Thief Gets Load of Goods," Alton Evening Telegraph (Alton, Illinois), Sep 28, 1909, Page 3

[235] "Foreign Coins in Plunder of Negro Slayers," St. Louis Post-Dispatch (St. Louis, Missouri) · Tue, Jan 16, 1906 · Page 6; "Murder at Granite City," Salem Herald-Advocate (Salem, Illinois) · Fri, Jan 19, 1906 · Page 6

[236] "Foreign Coins in Plunder of Negro Slayers," St. Louis Post-Dispatch (St. Louis, Missouri) · Tue, Jan 16, 1906 · Page 6; "Murder at Granite City," Salem Herald-Advocate (Salem, Illinois) · Fri, Jan 19, 1906 · Page 6

[237] "Two Go To Hospital," The Edwardsville Intelligencer (Edwardsville, Illinois) · Tue, May 19, 1908 · Page 1

[238] "Theft Report Shows Brothers' Amazing Thrift," St. Louis Post-Dispatch (St. Louis, Missouri) · Sat, Aug 14, 1909 · Page 3

[239] "Fake Dry Agents Rob Pickle Maker of $1900," St. Louis Post-Dispatch (St. Louis, Missouri) · Sun, Dec 8, 1929 · Page 17

[240] "Posing As Dry Agents Robbers Steal $1900," St. Louis Post-Dispatch (St. Louis, Missouri) · Sun, Feb 22, 1931 · Page 1

[241] "Couple of Pretty Good Fellows Rob 2 Granite City Theater Men," St. Louis Post-Dispatch (St. Louis, Missouri) · Tue, Mar 30, 1948 · Page 1

[242] "Long Nose Clue to Visitor Who Poisoned Five," St. Louis Post-Dispatch (St. Louis, Missouri) · Sun, Nov 22, 1908 · Page 18
[243] "Still Good Picking," The Edwardsville Intelligencer (Edwardsville, Illinois) · Tue, Aug 19, 1924 · Page 1, 7.
[244] "Still Good Picking," The Edwardsville Intelligencer (Edwardsville, Illinois) · Tue, Aug 19, 1924 · Page 1, 7.
[245] "Strike Puts Out Tri-City Lights," The St. Louis Star and Times (St. Louis, Missouri) · Thu, Mar 23, 1911 · Page 6
[246] "Dynamite Bomb Wrecks Truck of Bake Shop Owner," The St. Louis Star and Times (St. Louis, Missouri) · Thu, Dec 6, 1934 · Page 3
[247] "Macedonian Must Leave the Land of the Free," The Edwardsville Intelligencer (Edwardsville, Illinois) · Fri, Apr 30, 1909 · Page 1
[248] "Duelist is Fined $5.40," Alton Evening Telegraph (Alton, Illinois) · Fri, Mar 31, 1911 · Page 3
[249] "2 Die in Gun Duel in Drinking Place," Joplin Globe (Joplin, Missouri) · Tue, Sep 4, 1923 · Page 1
[250] "Shot in Brawl at Madison Bar," St. Louis Post-Dispatch (St. Louis, Missouri) · Mon, Sep 3, 1923 · Page 1
[251] "Slayer Confesses," The St. Louis Star and Times (St. Louis, Missouri) · Wed, Sep 27, 1911 · Page 12
[252] Stevens, Walter B., "St. Louis: The Fourth City, 1764-1909, Vol. 2," (Chicago-St. Louis: S.J. Clarke Publishing Co., 1909), Pg. 428.
[253] "St. Louisan Looks for Turkish War," St. Louis Post-Dispatch (St. Louis, Missouri) · Sun, Sep 20, 1903 · Page 3
[254] "Appeals for Aid," The Minneapolis Journal (Minneapolis, Minnesota) · Thu, Oct 8, 1903 · Page 5
[255] "Chicago Macedonians," Clarion-Ledger (Jackson, Mississippi) · Thu, Sep 17, 1903 · Page 1
[256] "Newspaper to Explain Liberty," St. Louis Post-Dispatch (St. Louis, Missouri) · Mon, Oct 7, 1907 · Page 4
[257] "Bulgarian Celebration," The Edwardsville Intelligencer (Edwardsville, Illinois) · Mon, Jan 20, 1908 · Page 1
[258] "10,000 Macedonians Meet and Send Telegram to Roosevelt," St. Louis Post-Dispatch (St. Louis, Missouri) · Mon, Apr 20, 1908 · Page 6
[259] "Men Kiss Each Other," Alton Evening Telegraph (Alton, Illinois), Oct 30, 1912, Page 7
[260] "Getting the War News," St. Louis Post-Dispatch (St. Louis, Missouri), Feb 9, 1913, Page 50
[261] "Hypnotism is Charged When a Witness Forgets," St. Louis Post-Dispatch (St. Louis, Missouri) · Sun, Jan 23, 1910 · Page 22
[262] "Hypnotism is Charged When a Witness Forgets," St. Louis Post-Dispatch (St. Louis, Missouri) · Sun, Jan 23, 1910 · Page 22

[263] "Bulgarian Band Reunited," St. Louis Post-Dispatch (St. Louis, Missouri) · Tue, Nov 30, 1915 · Page 2
[264] "Granite City Bulgarians Make Plebiscite Demand," The St. Louis Star and Times (St. Louis, Missouri) · Sat, Aug 30, 1919 · Page 3
[265] St. Louis Post-Dispatch (St. Louis, Missouri) · Sun, Nov 26, 1916 · Page 43
[266] St. Louis Post-Dispatch (St. Louis, Missouri) · Tue, May 9, 1911 · Page 18
[267] St. Louis Post-Dispatch (St. Louis, Missouri) · Mon, Mar 24, 1913 · Page 16
[268] St. Louis Post-Dispatch (St. Louis, Missouri) · Wed, Oct 19, 1910 · Page 14
[269] "Exonerates the Bulgarians," St. Louis Post-Dispatch (St. Louis, Missouri) · Tue, Oct 11, 1927 · Page 18
[270] "Madison Meeting of Macedonians To Open Sunday," The St. Louis Star and Times (St. Louis, Missouri) · Thu, Sep 1, 1938 · Page 12
[271] "Former Madison Man Killed in War in Spain," St. Louis Post-Dispatch (St. Louis, Missouri) · Tue, Nov 2, 1937 · Page 5
[272] "14th St. Mayor Shows How To Support the War," St. Louis Post-Dispatch (St. Louis, Missouri) · Sun, Aug 9, 1942 · Page 59
[273] "Bulgarian-American Calendar-Almanac for 1920," (Granite City: Naroden Glas, 1920), Pg. 158-159.
[274] Nikolovski-Katin, Slave, "The Macedonians in USA and Canada," (Skopje, 2002), Pg. 95.
[275] "Have a Wide Range," The Edwardsville Intelligencer, Edwardsville, Madison, Illinois Fri, Feb 26, 1909 · Page 1
[276] Cassens, David E., "The Bulgarian Colony of Southwestern Illinois, 1900-1920," *Illinois Historical Journal, Vol. 84*, (Spring 1991).

Made in the USA
Middletown, DE
12 January 2020